The Politics of Food

The Politics of Food

*The Global Conflict between Food
Security and Food Sovereignty*

WILLIAM D. SCHANBACHER

PRAEGER SECURITY INTERNATIONAL

 PRAEGER

AN IMPRINT OF ABC-CLIO, LLC
Santa Barbara, California • Denver, Colorado • Oxford, England

9/15/10
Lan
$ 34.95

Library of Congress Cataloging-in-Publication Data

Schanbacher, William D.
   The politics of food : the global conflict between food security and food sovereignty / William D. Schanbacher.
      p. cm.
   Includes bibliographical references and index.
   ISBN 978-0-313-36328-3 (alk. paper) — ISBN 978-0-313-36329-0 (ebook)
1. Food-supply—Political aspects.   2. Food-supply—Government policy.   I. Title.
   HD9000.6.S33   2010
   338.1'9—dc22   2009037033

ISBN: 978-0-313-36328-3
EISBN: 978-0-313-36329-0

14   13   12   11   10   1   2   3   4   5

This book is also available on the World Wide Web as an eBook.
Visit www.abc-clio.com for details.

Praeger
An Imprint of ABC-CLIO, LLC

ABC-CLIO, LLC
130 Cremona Drive, P.O. Box 1911
Santa Barbara, California 93116-1911

This book is printed on acid-free paper ∞

Manufactured in the United States of America

Contents

Introduction

Riots protesting the World Trade Organization (WTO) on the streets of Seattle in 1999, global demonstrations against the World Bank and International Monetary Fund (IMF), and civil unrest around the world due to rising food prices in 2008 all speak to a growing global awareness of and discontent with the fact that the basic necessity of food is not reaching hundreds of millions of people around the world each year.[1] These protests, marches, and often violent uprisings can be viewed, in part, as a growing chorus of voices speaking out against the political and economic policies by the world's affluent, industrialized countries and the global governance institutions that propagate these policies around the world. The creation of the World Bank and IMF in Bretton Woods, New Hampshire after the end of the World War II ushered in a new era of globalization that has culminated in forms of global governance that have left many asking: Who are the true beneficiaries of current models of globalization, and why do billions of people around the world continue to live in poverty despite World Bank and IMF promises to solve this problem?[2] Of particular importance with respect to these questions is the role food production, distribution, and consumption plays as an aspect of hunger and malnutrition.

Many multilateral organizations such as the World Bank, IMF, WTO, and the United Nations (UN) have utilized the term *food security* to describe the global effort to eliminate hunger and malnutrition. The effort to secure food for the global poor is, furthermore, intimately connected to the relationship between agricultural reform and small-scale, peasant, and landless farm production. These rural farmers are currently a central focus of certain policy agencies, such as the UN, due to the potential economic importance they hold for many developing countries. As such, small-scale farmers are at the heart of discussion regarding food security for the rural poor. Unfortunately, the theories and policies of the aforementioned multilateral organizations have not achieved their goals of curbing hunger, malnutrition, and global poverty, and, consequently, the world's farmers are among those who suffer the most. Given the failure to implement successful policies, the notion of food security needs further scrutiny on both theoretical and policy grounds.

The concept of food security emerged in the 20th century as post-WWII reconstruction efforts and the decolonization of many Third World countries created a global food regime that was managed through complex local, national, and international relations. With the creation of the IMF, World Bank, and more recently, the WTO, food security is increasingly sought through economic policies including trade liberalization, privatization, deregulation of national industry, and the opening of economic markets. The guiding principle for these multilateral institutions is the idea that economic growth, via market mechanisms, provides the most suitable solution for curbing poverty and achieving food security. However, critics of these strategies point to how a purely market-based approach to food security remains entrenched in neocolonial power structures that have failed to create a just global food system.

Although the World Bank and IMF are the most powerful lending agencies on a global level, they are not the only players involved in global financial governance. This book does not investigate regional banks such as the Inter-American Development Bank, but it is important to note that these regional banks play a powerful role in terms of regulating macroeconomic conditions in their respective regions. Ultimately, however, regional banks often ascribe to the same neoliberal economic theory of the World Bank and IMF. Moreover, the power structure, for example, of the Inter-American Development Bank is similar to the IMF and the World Bank. The United States carries enough voting power to effectively veto any bank decisions it does not agree with, and thus the potential for regional banks to challenge World Bank and IMF policies is drastically undermined.[3] In the end, neoliberal policies that underwrite World Bank, IMF, and regional bank decisions remain the fundamental problem with respect to food security.

Given these failures, an alternative concept and movement known as *food sovereignty* is garnering worldwide interest and support. A diverse amalgamation of small-scale, peasant, and landless farmers, rural workers, women, youth, and indigenous peoples, food sovereignty activists challenge both the theory that underlies the food security model and the policies that have emerged from it. This book offers an ethical analysis of the current food security model and the food sovereignty movement as they function within discourses on global poverty, hunger, and malnutrition. Focusing on these issues will also provide the context in which we can better understand the role food plays with respect to discussions on globalization and global poverty.

I argue that a critical analysis of the food security and food sovereignty models reveals fundamental antagonisms between the way hunger and malnutrition are conceived within these two constructs. Ultimately, the food security model is founded on, and reinforces, a model of globalization that reduces human relationships to their economic value. Alternatively, the food sovereignty model considers human relations in terms of mutual dependence, cultural diversity, and respect for the environment. Because food security has not been achieved for hundreds of millions of the world's poor, it is imperative that the food sovereignty model take center stage in the fight against global hunger and malnutrition. Furthermore, not only do we need to conceive of food as a human right, but, as food sovereignty argues, our definition of food should include the ways in which the poor deserve to have access to healthy, nutritious, and culturally important types of food. Given the massive amount of human suffering that goes on daily due to hunger and malnutrition, often unnoticed by the world's more well-off, the global food system is in desperate need of the same attention we give to other human rights issues such as genocide and terrorism. Ultimately, if food sovereignty's demands are not met, the current global food system constitutes a massive violation of human rights.

THE NEED FOR A UNIFIED FRONT AGAINST GLOBAL HUNGER AND MALNUTRITION

Given the complex relationship between economic, political, and cultural forms of globalization, research and input from multiple disciplines is required for a nuanced and critical investigation of global hunger and poverty. Various academic, technical, and local perspectives all contribute to how we conceive of the global poor, and provide perspectives on how to craft strategies to eliminate hunger and poverty. This book offers an ethical examination of these issues, although in doing so also draws from other disciplines involved in researching and discussing global food concerns.

The fields of political science and economics contribute crucial insights on neoliberal and developmental economic theory and policy implemented by multilateral organizations such as the UN, World Bank, IMF, and WTO. In order to critically understand how these organizations address global poverty, one must look at factors such as how poverty is conceived; how World Bank Structural Adjustment Programs (SAPs) have influenced foreign and domestic macroeconomic policies; how the emergence of powerful transnational corporations (TNCs) has established new and amorphous boundaries between states, citizens, and industry; and how a free market system has concentrated wealth in certain economic sectors. Examining these issues is important because they provide a fruitful resource for analyzing themes such as sustainable economic growth and development, the relationship between food and poverty, and how macroeconomic policies have succeeded or failed in certain countries and regional contexts.

From an ethical perspective, there is increasing acknowledgment of the interrelation between economics, politics, and ethics. With respect to global hunger and malnutrition, this interconnection is most visible in the alternative perspectives presented by the food sovereignty movement. This movement advocates and embodies a local-, family-, and community-based ethic that stresses values of sustainability, interdependence, environmental protection, and local production for local consumption. To a certain extent these values are increasingly at odds with an industrialized, corporate-driven rationale of individual autonomy, profiteering, and unfettered consumption. Ethicists are progressively demanding that the discipline of ethics should not be relegated to the sidelines in favor of more scientific disciplines. Rather, ethics should be considered a viable, foundational perspective from which we approach problems associated with hunger and global poverty. In other words, ethical discussions on globalization and poverty should not be confined to how poverty can be eliminated *given* current trends in global integration, but should also include how the existence of poverty is created and perpetuated by certain political, economic, and corporate policies that can be contravened.

The ethical proposals contained in the final two chapters are pragmatic in nature. Topics of social justice and economic, social, and political equality are central themes within these chapters; however, I do not attempt to offer a grand ethical theory of justice or equality. Rather, following a remark by economist Amartya Sen, this project aims to contribute to "making the world less unjust rather than attempting to articulate a grand theory of justice."[4] While theories of justice are imperative for providing the philosophical foundations for why those concerned with social justice pursue the things they do, a practical investigation of the current global food system requires both a certain level of idealism and some concrete policy options that can be implemented to alleviate the world's hungry and malnourished. The food sovereignty model includes both an idealism and a practicality that is required for tackling problems associated with hunger, poverty, and globalization.

Ultimately, food sovereignty is based on the hope that the global food system can be organized in such a way that the basic dignity of all humanity is restored. This hope is not unique. The Preamble to the United Nation's Declaration of Human Rights, for example, notes that all people are united by our common humanity, which is rooted in the inherent dignity and "equal and inalienable rights of all members of the human family."[5] In other words, human dignity serves as the founding concept upon which all other aspects of human rights are based. However, the concept of dignity in the Declaration remains rather vague in nature and thus requires a certain level of substantiation. To address this issue, Martha Nussbaum's list of basic human capabilities proves particularly useful. Living a life of dignity requires first and foremost that people have adequate basic necessities that allow them to lead a normal life free of hunger, malnutrition, and premature death. But there is also more to dignity.

As humans, we have the unique capacity to use our creative energies, both mental and physical. We produce literary, musical, and artistic works, we build homes and gardens, and we cultivate the earth's natural resources to provide sustenance for our families. Our creative productions are expressions of our physical senses, our ability to reason, and our imagination. As such, a meaningful life of dignity requires basic social and political arrangements that allow us to fully develop our creative capacities. The only way to ensure this is through basic political freedoms, including freedom of expression, freedom of assembly, and freedom of conscious. The food sovereignty movement recognizes this interconnection between human dignity, basic freedoms, and creative production, and draws attention to how an agrarian life is more than simply harvesting crops for sale on the global market. Instead, farming is a way of life that is intimately tied to familial and community relationships, religious beliefs and traditions, and a deep-seeded respect for the environment.

A life of dignity also involves the ability "to recognize and show concern for other humans" by developing social networks, meaningful friendships, and intimate relationships.[6] Humans are social in nature, yet we often dismiss the extent to which we are interconnected and mutually dependent on each other. Food sovereignty activists inscribe this fundamental aspect of humanity into their struggle for social justice by reminding us that we are not simply self-interested, autonomous, competitive beings. Instead, we find joy in our ability to laugh, play, and participate in recreational activities. Farmer movements such the *Campesino a Campesino* (Farmer to Farmer), which embrace the food sovereignty cause, embody these aspects of human dignity by demonstrating how farming communities are founded on community gatherings, the exchange of knowledge, and social events that express the cultural traditions of an agrarian livelihood.

Although the idea of human dignity is foundational in human rights documents such as the Declaration of Human Rights, the food sovereignty movement provides concrete expressions of the dignity of the world's small-scale, peasant, and landless famers. Ultimately, however, the aforementioned aspects of human dignity all depend on whether people have basic necessities such as adequate food. If people suffer from malnutrition and hunger on a daily basis, they by no means have this opportunity.

CHAPTER DESCRIPTIONS

Chapter one analyzes the notion of food security deployed by organizations such as the United Nation's Food and Agricultural Organization (FAO) and the International Fund for Agricultural Development (IFAD), as well as multilateral organizations including the World Bank, the International

Monetary Fund (IMF), and the World Trade Organization (WTO). While the WTO, World Bank, and IMF do not offer a systematic definition of food security, they deserve special attention given their direct influence upon global economic management and integration. Focusing specifically on production, distribution, and consumption patterns illustrates how food security is conceived and theorized both explicitly and implicitly within these institutions, and introduces the way food security falls somewhere along the spectrum of developmental and neoliberal models of globalization. Although this chapter ultimately argues that neoliberal, free-market economic concepts such as trade liberalization, deregulation, privatization, and growth still remain the dominant ethos of multilateral organizations, developmental approaches have identified past failures of World Bank, IMF, and WTO policies, and thus have begun reformulating strategies to more adequately attend to these failures.

On an analytical level, what is important about examining how these organizations conceive of global poverty in general, and food security as an aspect of global poverty in particular, is the fact that there is a spectrum of theory and policy. Developmental economic approaches utilized primarily by the FAO and IFAD have adjusted to past failures of many World Bank, IMF, and WTO policies, and have recognized that the effort to achieve food security must involve greater levels of sustainable development, agricultural reform, and coordination with the agricultural communities affected by policy. Indeed, even the World Bank, IMF, and WTO have recognized many failures of past policy and have begun, at least on a rhetorical level, to reconsider how their policies should be reformulated in the future. With that said, however, this chapter demonstrates that, on a foundational level, food security remains entrenched in a particular conception of human relations, a conception that understands the human qua human as *homo economicus*, or the economic man. The principle aim of highlighting this conception of humanity, which will be clarified in chapters three and five, is to demonstrate how this conception not only influences the nature of policy, but perhaps more importantly, reflects a notion of human relations that is contestable. After investigating these themes, a brief historical overview provides the contextual conditions, such as the rise of developmental economic growth paradigms, for what is now coined the global politics of food.

Chapter two investigates critical issues associated with how these multilateral organizations conceive of and implement policy for food security. This analysis presents counter arguments to multilateral financial and trade policy by examining the concrete successes and failures of these organizations' policies. Developmental policies promoted by the FAO and IFAD have made progress in terms of linking development workers with local communities in an effort to create more sustainable practices of agricultural production. Documents from the FAO and IFAD also reveal a concerted effort to include development communities in the process of development. Strategies such as microfinance, for example, have been implemented in certain regions and in particular contexts to help build rural financial infrastructure as well as educate rural peoples on how to manage finances for future use. To this extent, the food security model conceived by UN agencies holds much potential. However, critical examination of these organizations' documents also reveals that knowledge sharing between UN field workers and their rural counterparts remains managerial in nature. Despite increasing attempts to incorporate rural peoples in the development process, documents still appear dedicated to the idea that growth, competition, and profiteering are values necessary for a bolstered global economy. Although this is true to a certain extent, underlying this process is the question, to what end or purpose is developmental growth envisioned? These documents suggest that building rural infrastructure and educating farmers in methods of sustainable development is the first step in the larger goal of integrating the rural poor into global market relationships.

Following an examination of developmental approaches propagated by the FAO and IFAD is an interrogation of the policies pursued by the World Bank, IMF, and WTO. Historically these processes emphasized a neoliberal economic approach that ultimately proved detrimental to efforts to both reduce global poverty and to reduce hunger and malnutrition. WTO policies guided by World Bank and IMF-sponsored Structural Adjustment Programs (SAPs) will be analyzed to show how certain trade agreements asymmetrically benefited, and continue to benefit, industrialized, Northern economies such as the United States and Europe while at the same time created immense hardships, particularly for the rural poor in developing countries. World Bank strategies of agricultural reform, which were guided by principles of market-based reform, ultimately benefited the rural elite in developing contexts, as well as helped to establish the necessary conditions for the monopolization of certain agricultural sectors by transnational corporations (TNCs). Teasing out how food security is envisioned by these types of policies is complicated by the fact that the aims of many of these strategies were more centered on curbing global poverty in general rather than on providing food security. However, what is clear is the underlying economic conception of food security. Rather than conceiving of food as a cultural commodity intimately linked with particular values such as interdependence, cooperation, love of nature, and so forth, food is considered an abstract commodity with no inherent value.

In an effort to contextualize some of these critical issues, this chapter also provides case studies, including the repercussions of World Bank-sponsored structural adjustment programs on the Mexican tortilla industry, the problems associated with food aid as a solution to food insecurity, and the Monsanto Company as an example of the emerging role of TNCs. As evidence will show, these policies and organizations have not only failed to achieve global food security, but in many ways have exacerbated global hunger and poverty.

Chapter three offers an alternative to food security by introducing the concept of food sovereignty. As both a concept and a social movement, food sovereignty challenges current trends in economic, political, and cultural globalization. Focusing on organizations such as *La Via Campesina* and movements such as the *Campesino a Campesino* (Farmer to Farmer) movement, this chapter investigates critical issues and practices of food sovereignty, including themes of biodiversity, agroecology, and sustainable development. The food sovereignty movement is, on many levels, radically different than the food security approach and its attending understanding of globalization. Officially established in 1993, the movement is composed of peasants, farmers, small and medium-scale famers, rural women, and indigenous peoples. At its core, the food sovereignty movement fights for the human right to food and the right of peoples, countries, and states to define their agricultural and food policies. Alongside control over how food is produced, distributed, and consumed, the idea of sovereignty ultimately centers on local, state, and regional control over natural resources such as land and water. While these demands are not unproblematic, at its core, food sovereignty represents an alternative framework to global governance imposed by multilateral organizations. Food sovereignty contends that food security denigrates the cultural importance of food by considering food simply on the level of the caloric intake needed for human survival. Instead, according to food sovereignty, food represents a cultural commodity that much of the world regards in terms of its nutritive value, taste, and tradition; namely, a fundamental element of farmer and community livelihoods. Food sovereignty activists highlight the failures of multilateral economic policies and argue, for example, that the WTO should be banned from agriculture.

While this chapter introduces food sovereignty as an alternative to food security and its attending vision of globalization, what is ultimately illuminating is the contrasting vision of human relations embodied by food sovereignty. In contrast to themes of competition, efficiency, unfettered growth and consumption, autonomy, and profiteering, food sovereignty emphasizes themes of sustainable development, environmental conservation, genuine agricultural reform, mutual dependence, and local, small-scale community prosperity. By juxtaposing both neoliberal and developmental notions of food security, we begin to see a different understanding of the global food regime and how it plays a role in conceiving of and curbing global poverty. Although food sovereignty is its own social movement with its own specific demands, case studies on Brazil's Landless Workers Movement (MST), the Zapatista movement in southern Mexico, and the emerging international demand for biofuels provide context to some of these critical issues and practices. Ultimately, the food sovereignty movement argues that healthy, nutritious, and culturally important food is a *human right*, a right that obligates multilateral and state institutions to ensure its protection through more equitable land distribution and local production for local consumption.

Chapter four analyzes the ethical implications of food security and food sovereignty. It delineates the differences between food security and food sovereignty and highlights how food sovereignty presents an alternative to current, economic perspectives of globalization. Food sovereignty's emphasis on community, cooperation, sustainable development, and local knowledge is contrasted to corresponding neoliberal and developmental notions of individualism, competition, excessive consumption, and hierarchal, managerial knowledge. This chapter takes a detailed look at the issue of rights generally, and human rights specifically, and evaluates the United Nation's and food sovereignty's idea of food as a human right. One of the major debates within human rights discourse pertains to whether we can ethically justify a set of universal human rights. Criticisms of the concept of human rights often come from a cultural relativism perspective that argues that rights are based on particular human values. Because human values differ according to culture, location, and historical perspective, it is impossible to determine a universal standard of rights that applies to all peoples at all times. In an effort to address these criticisms, the UN has made progressive inroads into a more inclusionary understanding of cultural difference. As such, an examination of particular UN documents such as the International Covenant on Civil and Political Rights (ICCPR), and the International Covenant on Economic, Social, and Cultural Rights (ICESCR) is offered as a working example that serves to promote further dialogue regarding the debates between universalism and relativism with respect to human rights.

Within this discussion on human rights, this chapter also analyzes problems associated with the fulfillment of human rights. Traditionally, the language of rights centers on concepts of positive and negative rights and duties. After determining if and what sorts of rights people have, we must also identify who has a responsibility to fulfill them. Generally speaking, a positive rights/duties approach argues that people possess certain *a priori* rights and that it is up to individuals and governments to provide these rights. Alternatively, a negative rights/duties approach argues that people have rights that are limited to noninterference. Namely, people have the right to demand that individuals and governments do not interfere with respect to personal liberty, private property, and so on. This debate poses special problems for discussions on human rights and specifically rights associated with discussions on global poverty. The work of Thomas Pogge is offered as a fruitful perspective for understanding the status of human rights with respect to global poverty. Pogge orients a discussion on human rights around negative duties and argues that if we can demonstrate that affluent countries, and the global conditions they have helped to create and sustain, are infringing on people's negative rights, then those who implement and support these policies are involved in a massive violation of human rights. By conceiving of human rights in terms of negative rights and duties, Pogge presents a more rigorous and theoretically substantive foundation for the fight against global poverty.

This chapter concludes with some prescriptive ethical and policy suggestions by evaluating the work of Amartya Sen and Martha Nussbaum. Specifically, their respective versions of the capabilities approach are offered as a fertile theoretical ground from which to formulate policy for curbing global poverty and envisioning a more just world. The capabilities approach circumvents many of the problems associated with rights language and offers concrete examples of what it means to live a life of dignity. By utilizing concepts of human flourishing and human well-being, the capabilities approach may aid us in reconceptualizing how we approach human relationships generally, and global poverty specifically. Capabilities have a special role to play with respect to development because they outline basic human necessities as well as the conditions that are necessary for humans to flourish. Basing future policy on the capabilities approach aids developmental models by focusing attention on human values and desires beyond basic necessities.

Chapter five applies the ethical discussion of chapter four specifically to the food sovereignty movement. The values food sovereignty embodies both on a theoretical level and in its demands for new policy provides a substantive example of many of the ethical themes addressed in chapter four. However, food sovereignty also compels organizations such as the UN and state governments to rigorously formulate policy directly focused on providing the right to food. Although food sovereignty focuses on the specific issues of food and agriculture, its demands transcend this aspect of poverty and challenge us to re-envision how we conceive of the global poor. Additionally, the notion of human rights specifically presented by Pogge can aid food sovereignty in terms of making the demand for food more forceful. By demonstrating that current neoliberal models of food security, which fall under the general umbrella of neoliberal economic policy, constitute a violation of human rights, food sovereignty can, at least rhetorically, make its demand for the right to food more meaningful.

This chapter also provides some brief remarks on challenges the food sovereignty movement faces in the future. Recent analyses show that food sovereignty advocates need to clarify the differences between food security, food sovereignty, and food as a human right. In part, this project aims to aid in this effort, albeit through an examination of food security as it can be teased from the theory and policy of multilateral organizations. From an ethical perspective, Pogge's understanding of negative duties and human rights provides a helpful way in which food sovereignty might distinguish itself from food security. Namely, if it can be demonstrated that current food security models are complicit in a global order that fails to vigorously resolve problems of hunger and malnutrition, then it too constitutes a violation of human rights. Admittedly, this may only have force on a rhetorical level, but it still provides more content to food sovereignty's call for food as a human right.

Ultimately, contrasting themes of mutual well-being, a respect for the natural environment, and the sustainability of local, traditional forms of knowledge to a purely economic understanding of human relations presents an avenue of research that transcends the juxtaposition of food security and food sovereignty. In line with many of the ethical imperatives presented by food sovereignty, the ethic I propose shows that a sober assessment of current trends in economic globalization does not relegate social justice to the confines of idealism. Rather, reinvigorating a dedication to community, cooperation, and sustainable development, along with a concomitant struggle for political and economic justice, can potentially create new and creative ways in which to curb global hunger and poverty.

CHAPTER 1

Globalization, Development, Food Security, and the Emergence of a Global Food Regime

INTRODUCTION: GLOBALIZATION AND FOOD SECURITY

According to the report of the former Special Rapporteur on the right to food to the United Nations, Jean Zieglar noted that in 2004 the number of undernourished people across the world had increased to 840 million.[1] Moreover, the recent global financial crisis has resulted in a global food crisis that includes volatile food prices, which risks increasing this number.[2] Given this astonishing figure, part of the global project to eliminate hunger and curb poverty involves disentangling the myriad forces that contribute to this alarming trend. Within discussions pertaining to global hunger and malnutrition, the theme of *food security* has emerged as a common concern for diverse groups of international financial and trade institutions, food rights activists, nongovernmental organizations, and national governments. As mentioned in the introduction to this manuscript, the role of food production, consumption, and distribution falls somewhere within broader narratives on globalization and poverty. To the extent that food security is located within complex social, economic, political, and cultural contexts, it is difficult, if not impossible, to detach the role of food security from themes such as trade, agricultural reform, rural and economic development, and global poverty.

One way to begin sifting through these complex factors is to examine how organizations such as the United Nations (UN), International Monetary Fund (IMF), the World Bank, and the World Trade Organization (WTO) influence, whether directly or indirectly, both the way food is conceived as either an economic or cultural commodity and how food production, distribution, and consumption should operate on international, national, and local levels. Of these organizations, the UN and the World Bank have played a direct and integral role in the development and policy formulation of food security. With its inception after WWII, the World Bank sought to promote global economic development through increased economic integration. By breaking down national barriers, the Bank envisioned the creation of a more harmonious world order that would serve to bring Third World countries out of poverty through developing national economies, freeing trade, and educating governments in the tradition of classical economic theory. In its early years the Bank viewed itself as the organizational body that would provide guidelines for international aid and lending, collect and disseminate information, and provide technical assistance to member countries.[3] These efforts were tied to a basic ideological framework upon which the Bank's leaders "believed that they had uncovered a basic truth—the fundamental unity of the global, capitalist economy—and that they had an obligation to spread this truth to others, who would presumably recognize its value and embrace it."[4]

Along with the creation of the World Bank, the architecture of the IMF was also established at Bretton Woods. The IMF does not play a direct role in achieving food security, but it is important to the extent that it works closely with the World Bank. As Joseph Stiglitz notes, the World Bank is "devoted to eradicating poverty," while the IMF is concerned with providing global financial stability.[5] Although the IMF has evolved in its mission and philosophy since its inception, with respect to food security it can be critiqued alongside the World Bank.[6] For example, when the World Bank engaged in structural adjustment loans in the 1980s, it needed the approval of the IMF, and as Stiglitz notes, with "that approval came IMF-imposed conditions" on how loan recipients needed to craft macroeconomic policy. Furthermore, developing countries were constantly in need of help, and, as such, "the IMF became a permanent part of life in most of the developing world."[7] Consequently, the IMF's policies should be considered insofar as the Fund influences the economic conditions within which the goal of food security is pursued.

Similar to the World Bank, the Food and Agricultural Organization (FAO) was established in much the same spirit of tackling global poverty, albeit with a specific mission to create a more efficient and egalitarian global distribution of food. The FAO's first director-general, Sir John Boyd Orr, proposed that feeding the world's poor would not only create a safer world, one that could avoid catastrophes such as WWI and WWII, but could also bolster the global economy, thus raising everyone's standard of living.[8] It was in this spirit that the FAO's original directors sought to achieve food security for the world's poor. Currently, the FAO and International Fund for Agriculture and Development (IFAD) function as development agencies of the UN. In the discussion below, we will examine how each respective agency sees itself in terms of striving to achieve food security.

This chapter focuses on these organizations because their governance powers increasingly influence local and national economic and social policy with respect to food security. How food security is defined will become clearer as these organizations are scrutinized, but a few provisional remarks will draw attention to specific issues that influence the objective of achieving food security. The difficulty of clearly defining food security is twofold in nature: on the one hand, UN organizations such as IFAD and the FAO may conceive of, and thus prescribe policy for, food security in a different manner than organizations such as the World Bank. Moreover, financial governance and international trade arrangements often create additional obstacles to achieving food security. Given heated debate over the theory and policy of food security, these organizations constantly redefine the term. As such, a definition of food security must be gleaned from the theory and policy that these organizations outline in their reports on larger global issues pertaining to poverty, economic growth, agricultural reform, and so forth. The UN and World Bank focus on the two broad, underlying themes of globalization and poverty. Specifically, they focus on curbing poverty, with food production and distribution playing an integral role in this effort. In this context, food security should be envisioned as a project of economic and developmental globalization that is designed to help poor and underdeveloped countries. That is, theory and policy needs to focus on how growth will be most beneficial to the global poor.

Take, for example, the United Nations. In 2003, the United Nations Development Program (UNDP) devoted its thematic report to global poverty and announced its Millennium Development Goals (MDGs).[9] Derived from the UN Millennium Summit in September of 2000, part of this project included the goal of halving global poverty by the year 2015. As renowned economist Jeffrey Sachs notes, "The debate is not about whether growth is good or bad but whether certain policies—including policies that may lead to closer global integration—lead to growth; and whether those policies lead to the kind of growth that improves the welfare of poor people."[10]

A couple of distinctions emerge here. First, the Bank defines the poor as those who live under $1.25 a day, which is the benchmark of the global poverty-line. For institutions such as the Bank, pro-poor growth is best instituted through neoliberal economic theory based on the free market. Strategies such as trade liberalization, privatization, and deregulation are best suited for this endeavor. Alternatively, UN organizations such as IFAD and the FAO recognize globalization as a double-edged sword. On the one edge, a free market may benefit the poor if they are able to engage in the world market in a fair and equitable manner. Given that all market relations are imperfect, these organizations urge the need for certain regulation and management to help reduce the hardships that accompany the poor's transition into larger economic relations. On the other edge, an unregulated free market may prove disastrous to the poor as they do not have adequate access to resources and knowledge of free market economic theory.

This distinction is important for the concept of food security. For the global governance institutions, food security is primarily an issue of producing enough food to feed the world's poor. As such, we need strategies that produce food in the most efficient and cheap way possible. Once enough food is secured, we need a distributive paradigm that delivers food in the most efficient and cheap way possible. IFAD and the FAO challenge this approach, arguing that while we need to produce food efficiently and cheaply, the best way to do so is not necessarily through unregulated trade liberalization, privatization, and deregulation. Instead, we need to look at the ways traditional forms of farming and agricultural growth and development are harmed by these types of strategies. Consumption plays a greater role according to these agencies, and IFAD and the FAO stress the need to implement policies that enable the rural poor to develop economic foundations that allow them to produce and consume the types of food they deem culturally important. However, this point should not be overstated. The focus is still on the potential for *economic* growth through free market mechanisms to solve global hunger and malnutrition. If the market is used to promote pro-poor growth, then hunger and poverty can be curbed or eliminated. The remainder of this chapter takes a more in-depth look at these organizations in an effort to develop the concept of food security. While, ultimately, we will not be able to glean a homogeneous definition of food security, certain commonalities between all of these organizations provide a platform from which advocates of the concept of food sovereignty wage their critique.

The United Nation's three major organizations that oversee global food, development, and agriculture frameworks are the Food and Agriculture Organization (FAO), the International Fund for Agricultural Development (IFAD), and the World Food Program. The following sections will briefly outline the first two organizations and highlight major policy agendas set by these institutions as a means to paint a picture of how the UN views food security and developmental globalization.

THE INTERNATIONAL FUND FOR AGRICULTURE DEVELOPMENT (IFAD)

IFAD is a subsidiary of the UN and a special agency concerned with food and global poverty. Emerging from the 1974 World Food Conference, delegates determined that an

International Fund for Agricultural Development should be established immediately to finance agricultural development projects primarily for food production in the developing countries. One of the most important insights emerging from the conference was that the causes of food insecurity and famine were not so much failures in food production, but structural problems relating to poverty and to the fact that the majority of the developing world's poor populations were concentrated in rural areas.[11]

In accordance with this inaugural mission statement, IFAD's commitment is to work with the rural poor through governments, donors, and nongovernmental organizations (NGOs) in an effort to locate "country-specific solutions, which can involve increasing rural poor people's access to financial services, markets, technology, land and other natural resources."[12]

IFAD's "2007–2010 Strategic Framework" report outlines the agency's policy agenda for the short-term future as well as its conception of, and strategy for, global development and food security. Its strategy statement outlines six major areas of focus, which offer objectives to ensure that the rural poor have the skills and organization needed for successful development. IFAD stresses the need for bolstered and secure access to land and water, which involves a larger effort to manage natural resources and engage in conservation practices that will ensure the most productive use of land. Along these lines, IFAD also recognizes the need for improving agricultural technologies, which, along with the creation of a broad range of financial services, will serve to increase agricultural production and build a capital base.[13]

As a developmental program, IFAD's strategy demonstrates a particular conception of the relationship between development and natural and financial resources. Natural resources are considered a form of capital from which the rural poor derive the ability to produce. Conservation and resource management are imperative insofar as they protect the capital base from which growth and production thrive. By improving agricultural technologies, rural farmers and food producers gain knowledge of how to increase productivity and how to utilize more efficient production practices, which ultimately allow them to be more competitive producers in local, national, and international markets. Financial services bolster local economies and allow the poor to establish a more stable economic base from which to further draw resources to increase growth and productivity. By creating stronger economic foundations, rural farmers create opportunities to leave farming livelihoods to either increase economic stability through more lucrative off-farm jobs or engage in entrepreneurial ventures. Ultimately, these objectives aim to integrate rural economies into the global market. While securing access to land, water, and natural resources is imperative for improving rural infrastructure and subsequently providing food security, the most efficient and productive strategy for achieving these goals entails steady and guided global integration. As the rural poor, and, specifically, rural farmers engage in these practices, they will simultaneously bolster food security as well as gain a foothold in the global economy.

Ultimately, this concept of development can be characterized as one in which the poor become *economically* self-sustaining. As an example of this particular conception of growth and development, one of IFAD's policy strategies includes the promotion of microfinance institutions (MFIs), which provide the poor with loans, access to financial services, and the opportunity

to establish local financial institutions. However, as IFAD notes, "microfinance is business not charity," and thus MFIs must strive to make a profit
and finance expansion through profitability. Furthermore, "only those MFIs
that have demonstrated their capacity for resource mobilization, cost coverage, profitability, and dynamic growth deserve assistance."[14] MFIs serve
to create and strengthen local markets by establishing financial infrastructure, creating and sustaining a capital base, and providing advice and training with respect to national and global economic trends. Conceptually, MFIs
envision growth as that which enables the poor (specifically the rural poor)
to become self-sustainable.[15]

The purpose of rural finance is to increase the productivity, income and food security of the rural poor by promoting access to sustainable financial services. IFAD
will strengthen the capacity of rural financial institutions to mobilize savings, have
their costs covered and loans repaid, and make a profit to increase their saver and
borrower outreach . . . Through its policy and strategies, IFAD confirms its commitment to continually seeking more effective ways of enabling—and empowering—
the rural poor to create a sustainable means of livelihood for themselves and for the
generations to come.[16]

While on the surface policy prescriptions such as MFIs seem laudable,
we must also ask how these strategies establish and advocate a particular
notion of development and food security. One way of approaching this
question involves deciphering how organizations such as IFAD understand
the notion of knowledge management. In general, knowledge management
refers to the idea that strategies for successful development require input
from a diverse chorus of voices, whether developmental institutions such
as IFAD, global governance institutions such as the WTO, World Bank, and
IMF, or rural farmers. Specifically, IFAD's proposal for knowledge management seeks to enable the rural poor to overcome poverty through "developmental practice." Supplementing its "Strategic Framework," IFAD's
strategy for knowledge sharing strives to share "information and knowledge related to rural poverty in order to promote good practice, scale up
innovations, and influence policies."[17]

While IFAD recognizes the failure of previous attempts by organizations such as the World Bank to institute strategies of "knowledge transfer"
in which rich countries *impart* knowledge (in terms of technology, agricultural development, etc.) to poor countries, the lessons learned from
previous failures still reveal a particular understanding of globalization,
and thus growth and development.[18] Here, globalization is conceived primarily as an economic phenomenon, whereby the success of growth and
development policies depend on how successful rural farmers are at assimi-
lating to global trade relations, how successful they are at utilizing technology and efficient modes of agricultural production, and so forth.

With respect to knowledge management, previous World Bank strategies asserted that the most efficient form of knowledge transfer was a

managerial form in which the Bank essentially imposed the theory and policy behind rural development projects. In the past, because rural farmers were ill-equipped to utilize advances in agricultural technologies, had a limited knowledge of free market economic theory, and lacked the resources (capital, land, etc.) needed for efficient production, global institutions such as the World Bank were required to coordinate this effort. However, this managerial or top-down form of knowledge management drew criticism as rural farmers began to voice discontent with being denied the opportunity to participate in development policy.

IFAD's current knowledge management strategy seeks to address these concerns. IFAD notes that current trends in trade liberalization, the evolving structure of agri-food chains, and the rising demand for biofuels, among other issues, present both opportunities and risks for the global poor and rural farmers. Knowledge management and sharing will thus involve a concerted effort to navigate these evolving global trends, or "old ways and methods that no longer respond to changed realities on the ground."[19] While IFAD's strategy of knowledge management appears to be a genuine attempt to incorporate rural farmers in development strategy discussions, what is illuminating is how it still holds a particular conception of "evolving global trends." Namely, strategies such as microfinancing reveal that, instead of critically challenging neoliberal economic theories of competition, efficiency, and growth for profit, IFAD seeks to use these theories to benefit the poor. As such, IFAD is committed to helping the rural poor by enabling them to assimilate to the global economy.

As an aspect of food security, the goal is, on the one hand, to work with rural farmers in an effort to gain knowledge of agricultural practices, and on the other, to offer strategic suggestions on how rural farmers can best assimilate to changes in the global economy. Similar to Sachs's notion of pro-poor development, IFAD seeks to make the transition from self-sustainable farming and food production to larger economic relations as beneficial and harmless as possible for the poor. Food security in this sense is not regarded as a fundamental critique of current economic theory and policy, but rather as a practical strategy for improving the livelihoods and productive capacities of the rural poor. While IFAD's strategies represent one perspective of globalization and developmental growth, the following chapters challenge this perspective precisely on the grounds that it does not vigorously question the ways in which developmental economic theory remains wedded to neoliberal concepts of competition, efficiency, and profiteering.

THE UN AND THE FOOD AND AGRICULTURE ORGANIZATION

Along with IFAD, the FAO is one of the most influential research and development arms of the United Nations. In its 2006 report "The State of

Food Security in the World," the FAO reiterated many of the same concerns of the 2003 UN Human Development Report (Millennium Development Goals); namely, it stated that "reducing hunger is no longer a question of means in the hands of the global community."[20] According to this report, the world was richer than it was 10 years previously, there was enough food available (and more that could be produced) to feed the world, and research and technology had progressed to the point where it could tackle the major problems associated with global hunger. Despite setbacks, the FAO contended that eradicating global hunger could be achieved, and that the most pressing issue involved the "political will to mobilize those resources to the benefit of the hungry."[21] Food security is less a problem of production as it is an issue of distribution and national governments' commitment to institute social and economic policies to ensure that adequate food resources reach the hungry. Part of this political willpower involves understanding current global economic trends and crafting policy that utilizes these trends to the advantage of the poor. These economic trends will become clearer as we examine the policies of the WTO, IMF, and World Bank, but for time being, it is important to note that, similar to IFAD, the FAO seeks to achieve food security through a pro-poor growth and development model.

In addressing poverty and hunger the FAO offers a "twin track approach," in which poverty will be reduced only if rural and agricultural reform plays a prominent role. Although the FAO recognizes the importance of context specific research and policy implementation (i.e. depending on region, geography, etc.), it offers some general guidelines for the future. If the MDGs are to be met, hunger reduction is paramount for accelerating development and poverty reduction. Agricultural growth is crucial. Moreover, the utilization of new technologies should focus primarily on the development of small-scale agriculture. With respect to building economic infrastructure, trade can serve to benefit the agricultural poor as long as state governments implement social safety nets to facilitate any harmful transitions into global market trade arrangements. Accordingly, the FAO argues that trade liberalization is not always the best policy in certain contexts.[22]

In pursuing these objectives, several policy goals must be accomplished. Programs must focus on global "hotspots," which contain the populations most affected by poverty and hunger. Given the fact that many of these regions are rural, agricultural reform must focus on pro-poor development and assistance in the form of social safety nets, health interventions, and food and nutrition programs. As a part of the agricultural reform effort, programs must seek to bolster private investment, and part of this process includes *making trade work for the poor*. Furthermore, national and institutional reform in the form of food for aid can play an influential role in this effort. And, finally, these goals must garner the continued support of the international community, and, most pressingly, the commitment of donor

countries to consign 0.7 percent of their gross national product to development assistance.

The FAO's expansive policy agenda provides a vision for the future of
rural and agricultural development that falls within a traditional, developmental food security model. Sustained food security requires a multilateral approach that includes political fidelity to growth and trade, as
well as economic integration of the rural poor. These reforms must include
a broad range of policy suggestions that focus primarily on developmental economic modeling with a specific emphasis on agricultural growth.
Although agricultural growth must focus on small-scale production, it is
up to developed countries to assist production through the introduction
of advanced agricultural technologies and strategies for optimizing economic competitiveness. As previously mentioned, part of bolstering rural
agricultural growth requires making trade advantageous to the rural poor.
Current trends in economic globalization are thus viewed as opportunities for achieving food security. There are still risks involved with transitioning from traditional models of rural farming and food production, but
with the help of social safety nets and aid from developed countries, these
transition costs can be minimized. Farmers need assistance learning new
agricultural techniques as well as how to employ modern agricultural technologies. Furthermore, farmers need to develop a greater knowledge of
global-agricultural trends in order to produce crops that will be competitive
on the global market. Similar to IFAD, the FAO prescribes broad policy
strategies that attempt to integrate the global poor into the global economy. The FAO's focus is less on how neoliberal and developmental economic theory/policy has contributed to hunger and poverty than on how
globalization can benefit the poor through the implementation of new policies. Again, the questions addressed in the following chapters pertain to
how IFAD and the FAO fail to address some of the deeper issues of economic globalization. By avoiding a more rigorous critique of neoliberal
and developmental economic theory, IFAD and the FAO remain married
to the belief that economic growth, competition, efficiency, and profiteering hold the answer to achieving food security.

To better understand the economic trends underpinning policy prescriptions by organizations such as IFAD and the FAO, policy makers and food
rights activists need to examine the current evolution and influence of
global governance bodies such as the WTO, World Bank, and the IMF. While
these organizations are not founded specifically for the purposes of providing food security, their global influence and visions of economic growth
and development play direct roles in how food security is conceived.

THE WTO, WORLD BANK, AND IMF

The IMF, World Bank, and WTO have respective spheres of influence in
propagating a certain vision of economic and social globalization. While

these organizations are under constant scrutiny, to understand how they influence food security, it is important to examine, first, their respective roles in global economic governance, and second, how they contribute to advocating particular strategies for rural growth and development. Part of the difficulty of ascertaining how these organizations conceive of food security is witnessed by the fact that they do not center policy prescriptions specifically on food security; rather, they discuss food security in the context of larger economic and political trends. However, reviewing their respective understandings of neoliberal economic globalization, global poverty and hunger, and agricultural growth allows us to glean an understanding of food security. As mentioned in the introduction to this chapter, these organizations diverge from IFAD and the FAO in their emphasis on trade liberalization, privatization, and deregulation. The neoliberal economic model based on efficiency, competition, profit maximization, and a free market provides the context for achieving food security.

THE WTO

Of the three major global governance bodies, the WTO is the most influential in managing global trade arrangements, which also affect agricultural policies. As such, the WTO plays an indirect role in the success of food security policies insofar as trade arrangements potentially impact global production and distribution of food. According to its mission statement, the WTO's main function is "to ensure that trade flows as smoothly, predictably and freely as possible" between nations.[23] To examine how the WTO envisions and influences food security, we may start with the inception of trade and agricultural policy proposals initiated under the General Agreement on Tariffs and Trade (GATT) and later developed in the Agreement on Agriculture during the Uruguay Round from 1986 to 1994. GATT was established after WWII as a forum for negotiating trade agreements and treaties, but originally excluded agriculture. However, in a series of trade talks during the Uruguay Round, trade issues covering services, intellectual property, and agriculture were added to negotiations. After the creation of the WTO, these negotiations continued, and in the 2001 Doha development round tensions flared. During these discussions, the WTO, along with the FAO, initiated a groundbreaking plan to reconceive trade arrangements, global economic integration, and agricultural governance. With respect to governance, the WTO reaffirmed its position as the ultimate authority in global trade negotiations and policy implementation. In its November 2001 Ministerial Conference, it declared that "the World Trade Organization has contributed significantly to economic growth, development and employment throughout the past fifty years."[24] To ensure that developing countries (the majority of WTO members) received "commensurate" benefits of growth and development projects, the Board avowed that the WTO was "the unique forum for global trade rule-making and liberalization, while also recognizing that regional trade agreements can play an important role in promoting the liberalization and expansion of trade and in fostering development." In asserting its position as the definitive authority, the WTO affirmed its commitment to working with the Bretton Woods (IMF, World Bank) institutions "for greater coherence in global economic policy making."[25] This coherence involved a coordinated effort on the part of the IMF, World Bank, and state governments to establish a unified vision of the global economy (even if regional contexts differed with respect to particular economic issues) as well as the trade arrangements that would be most beneficial to developing countries.

While the WTO recognizes that reconstructing trade arrangements is not always a fluid and successful process, overall, given the complexity of our current world, a global trade forum is necessary to direct the economic aspects of trade.[26] However, since the 2001 round, the Doha initiative has faced increasing criticism. The 2003 Cancun round was stalled due to disagreements on agricultural issues, and subsequent meetings in Singapore (2003) and Hong Kong (2005) failed to resolve these disputes.[27] The Doha reforms reached an indefinite stalemate at the Potsdam conference as the United States, European Union, India, and Brazil could not come to agreement on trade liberalization in certain countries.

The stalemate at Potsdam is characteristic of many agriculture trade disputes. Specifically, many member states challenge the 2001 declaration in which the WTO ostensibly committed to "negotiations" aimed at "substantial improvements in market access; reductions of, with a view to phasing out all forms of export subsidies; and substantial reductions in trade-distorting domestic support."[28] Under specific scrutiny is what the WTO terms "development boxes." Organized along color coded categories, the WTO identifies non-trade distorting subsidies (Green Box), subsidies that need to be reduced or phased out (Amber Box) and trade-distorting subsidies (Red Box), which also need to be eliminated.[29] The following chapter offers a more detailed analysis of these developmental boxes, but what should be noted is how the WTO sees these categories as a helpful framework for economic structural adjustment and economic integration. Identifying trade-distorting subsidies and domestic supports is an important aspect of the WTO policy agenda, but as critics point out, many powerful industrialized nations have been able to circumvent WTO regulations by manipulating the language that describes different types of supports or subsidies. Ultimately, however, the fundamental theory underscoring the WTO's vision of trade remains the same. Namely, the elimination or reduction of trade-distorting subsidies will ensure a more fair/free market, which will result in the ability for local and national economies to compete in the global marketplace. And more specifically, relating to agriculture, the reduction of trade-distorting subsidies will allow the least developed and developing countries to direct their agricultural markets (as well as all national markets) simultaneously toward foreign investment and export-oriented trade relationships.

Alongside trade liberalization, the Doha round also outlined a strategic framework for intellectual property rights and foreign investment by introducing the Trade-Related Intellectual Property Rights Agreement (TRIPS) and the Trade-Related Investment Measures (TRIMS). The original commitment to the "protection of traditional knowledge and folklore, and other relevant new developments raised by the Members pursuant of Article 71.1" remains the official position of the WTO.[30] Originally, in the construction of TRIPS, "new internationally-agreed trade rules for intellectual property rights were seen as a way to introduce more order and predictability, and for disputes to be settled more systematically."[31] In accordance with the WTO's commitment to be a rule-governing forum, the implementation of the TRIPS agreement provides least developed and developing countries with a venue for bringing disputes before the international community—a strategy that enables consensus on proper policy formulation and a standard by which all member countries must adhere. Ideally, the TRIPS agreement protects domestic corporate innovations and provides legal sanction for infractions by other nations and corporations. Coinciding with TRIPS regulations, TRIMS were conceived during the Doha round to bolster trade and investment, competition, and governmental transparency. Coupled with trade liberalization, the opening up of domestic markets to foreign investors and corporations, regulations such as TRIMS, according to the WTO, ensure a more stable and fair economic foundation upon which developing countries can enter the global economic market. Moreover, by opening up developing countries' markets to foreign investment, the TRIMS agreement facilitates the movement of foreign corporations into developing economies and, as a result, strengthens development and growth.

Alongside these specific structural features of the Doha negotiations, another strategy introduced and implemented in subsequent rounds was the concept of aid for trade. According to the WTO, aid for trade is a concept and strategy that allows developing countries with supply-side food constraints to benefit from the current multilateral trading system.[32] Given that developing countries inevitably experience adjustment lags, the WTO recognizes the need for aid that "finances trade-related technical assistance, trade-related infrastructure and aid to develop productive capacity."[33] According to the WTO, "The Doha Round of multilateral trade negotiations, launched in 2001, set out to address part of this problem [structural adjustment lags] by aiming to reduce trade-restricting and distorting practices that developing countries and LDCs [least developed countries] face in their main developed-country export markets and in South-South trade."[34] According to the WTO, aid for trade must address two issues: WTO members must help developing countries implement policies conducive to multilateral trade and help these countries adjust to economic lags that may result from the transition into global trade arrangements. Ultimately, the idea is that aid for trade incentives serve to attract developing countries to WTO standards and trade arrangements. By restructuring certain macroeconomic policies, developing countries can take optimum advantage of trade liberalization. With respect to agriculture, developing countries can, on the one hand, begin to produce food goods that are in high demand and, on the other, benefit from cheaper food imports from developing countries with surplus reserves.

The FAO has warned the WTO of potential dangers of trade liberalization, but still recognizes the potential for trade to bolster developing agricultural sectors. For instance, the FAO notes that "agricultural trade and trade liberalization can unlock the potential of the food and agricultural sector to stimulate growth and promote food security."[35] With respect to the initial Doha round of trade negotiations, both the WTO and the FAO advanced agricultural reform that not only accepted a developmental economic theory of growth and liberalization, but also made policy recommendations based on this model. With respect to the original Doha commitments, the question was not whether continued global market integration was appropriate, but how least developed countries could successfully benefit from integration. As far as the FAO was concerned, "the objective of reducing hunger and alleviating poverty through sustainable agriculture and rural development is not incompatible with the goal of establishing a 'fair and market-oriented agricultural trading system.'"[36] In attempting to reach this goal, the FAO recommended the following guiding definition of food security:

Food security at the individual, household, national, regional and global level will be achieved when all people, at all times, have physical and economic access to sufficient, safe and nutritious food to meet their dietary needs and food preferences for an active and healthy lifestyle.[37]

Statements such as this identify the need for safe and nutritious food, and also underscore the method by which to achieve this goal. Ultimately, food security will be achieved through economic integration based on a WTO (and IMF and World Bank) model. Again, this model focuses on trade liberalization through the opening up of domestic markets and the reduction of trade-distorting subsidies. Market access provides developing countries with the potential to deliver goods, and specifically agricultural exports, to the world market through competitive and specialized advantage. To achieve these goals, it is necessary to establish a rule-making forum—the WTO—to direct these efforts. While the WTO serves as the primary forum for trade related issues, its model of global development would be incomplete without the additional financial coordination of the World Bank and the IMF.

THE WORLD BANK

To understand the World Bank's contribution to food security, one must look first at the institution's primary function. The World Bank is currently a consortium of 185 countries that serves to provide financial and technical assistance to developing countries. One of the prominent strategies utilized by the World Bank in the last 30 years is the development of Structural Adjustment Programs (SAPs). While SAPs have proved both successful and disastrous depending on region and historical circumstance, what is important presently is the current structure of policy strategies. Generally speaking, SAPs are intended to bring national macroeconomic conditions to a place where the country in question can benefit from regional and international trade arrangements. As Walden Bello summarizes, "typically SAPs begin with stabilization measures such as tightening the money supply, letting interest rates rise, reducing government spending, and cutting wages."[38] This usually results in macroeconomic contraction, with the idea that austerity measures will allow national economies to reduce balance of payment deficits. For nations to successfully join the global market, they must first initiate domestic policies that will enable global economic integration. With respect to food security and agricultural reform, SAPs prove more complex. SAPs generally influence agriculture through specific reform policies that seek to optimize output, specialize crop production to accommodate market demand, and provide capital intensive methods of production (which usually are chemical and fertilizer intensive).

On a more specific food security level, the World Bank enacted its "From Vision to Action" report in 1997 as an attempt to articulate rural development strategies as a way to improve food security and direct economic growth. While the Bank admits that its initial strategies did not accomplish all of their goals, it rededicated its efforts in 2001 with the inception of a new program and strategy, "Reaching the Rural Poor," which "stresses practice, implementation, monitoring, and empowerment of the people it is designed to help."[39]

Similar to many IMF and WTO policy strategies, the primary focus of "Reaching the Rural Poor" is "broad based economic growth" that centers on rural agriculture. The Bank concedes that increasing global integration and economic liberalization creates risks as well as benefits for the poor, and thus, one of the major challenges is to find ways to "harness growth opportunities while managing risks and compensating losers."[40] To accomplish these goals, the Bank's proposals for rural development include strategies to foster broad-based and sustainable agricultural growth. Moreover, agricultural growth will depend largely on enhancing agricultural productivity both through natural resource management and agricultural competitiveness. Development must also focus on fostering nonfarm economic growth.

Pursuing these objectives requires stable national macroeconomic conditions and institutional frameworks that sustain growth.[41] Given the potential for developing nations to export agricultural products, one of the main conditions for enhancing growth involves the reduction or elimination of trade-distorting subsidies for developing nations to ensure that products can compete on a global level. As such, the Bank encourages increased trade liberalization in both industrialized and developing nations as a way to ensure that the global market is level for all countries.[42] Enhancing agricultural productivity involves enabling the rural poor to produce food goods that are competitive in the international market. While this may involve transitioning from traditional to market demanded or specialized cropping preferences, with the aid of agricultural technologies (including capital inputs, high-yield seed varieties, fertilization, etc.) rural farmers will not only be able to produce foods that generate more income, they will also benefit in the long run from the knowledge gained from these technologies.

Another aspect to alleviating poverty and hunger and enhancing agricultural productivity is the ability of developing countries to adapt to changing economic and globalization conditions; namely, developing countries must endorse domestic policies that "allow domestic producers to respond to domestic and foreign [economic] conditions."[43] The idea that developing nations must react to changing domestic and foreign conditions is a contentious issue that we must keep in mind when the following chapters challenge the presupposition that our current trends of economic globalization are inevitable. However, as far as the Bank is concerned, current forms of global integration are here to stay, and the best strategy for improving agricultural productivity and food security is to enable rural farmers and mitigate transition effects as they shift into larger economic networks.

In conjunction with IMF and WTO strategies, the Bank also highlights the need for sound governance and institutional frameworks. According to the Bank's research, "overcentralized institutional structures," which discourage the potential for foreign development investment, need to be reduced.[44] As decentralization processes continue, national governments and international organizations must remain dedicated to easing the burden on the poor through social services, participatory policy making, and pro-poor growth.

Because agricultural productivity is viewed as the primary means of escaping poverty, the Bank recommends a renewed vision of productivity and competitiveness. The new agenda must shift emphasis from "a narrow agricultural focus to a broader policy context," from "a focus on crop and livestock yields to market demands and incomes," from "staples to high value crops," and from "primary production to the entire food chain."[45] The Bank suggests that success will come with open agricultural economies, foreign direct investment, land reform, and rapid technological progress, among other factors.[46] As such, these agricultural policies follow the traditional SAP model, which requires the agricultural sector to align with larger national macroeconomic policies of adjustment.

These efforts have culminated in the Bank's 2008 Annual Report, which is dedicated specifically to agricultural development.[47] Reinforcing many of the policy strategies found in "Reaching the Rural Poor," the 2008 report addresses agriculture in terms of sustainable growth and development and meeting the Millennium Development Goals of halving poverty by 2015. With respect to agriculture and food security, the Bank's strategies can be expressed in its mission statement: "Using agriculture as the basis for economic growth in the agriculture-based countries requires a productivity revolution in small holder farming."[48]

This process involves a concerted effort by local, national, and global governance institutions to reform agriculture in a way that benefits smallhold farming. As a unique aspect of improving growth and development, agriculture can contribute to reducing poverty and hunger in several ways. First, as an "economic activity," agriculture can be a "provider of investment opportunities for the private sector, and a prime driver of agriculture-related industries and the rural nonfarm economy."[49] As a contributor to food security, agriculture should be understood insofar as it is a source of income, or a means for the rural poor to direct agricultural production toward more economically viable foods. Second, agriculture functions as "a livelihood" to the extent that it provides jobs to upwards of 1.3 billion smallholders and landless workers.[50] Finally, agriculture can potentially serve to improve environmental degradation. While rural agriculture is a large contributor to water depletion, agrochemical pollution, soil exhaustion, and so forth, it can also be managed in a way that preserves biodiversity and protects against natural disasters and climate change.[51]

Ultimately, the Bank's vision of the relation between agriculture and development is founded on the belief that countries "follow evolutionary paths" that can move them from poverty to self-sustainability through "classifying regions according to their agricultural potential."[52] While strategies vary according to country and region, what are definitively important are strategies that allow smallholders to "deliver surpluses to food markets and share in the benefits of expanding markets."[53] However, according to the Bank's estimates, agriculture has been vastly underused for development purposes. As such, agricultural productivity must assimilate to new and emerging global economic conditions. Part of this effort involves land reform whereby land markets attempt to raise productivity, help households diversify incomes, and facilitate exit from agriculture.[54] According to the Bank, these outcomes are desirable given that "well functioning land markets are needed to transfer land to the most productive users" whereby smallholders can gain "entry into the market" and "increase efficiency."[55] Moreover, improving "the productivity, profitability, and sustainability of smallholder farming" is the main pathway out of poverty.[56]

While the "Reaching the Rural Poor" document also recognizes the need for multilateral coordination and an increased participatory role of rural peasants and farmers, what is important for current analysis is the broad picture the World Bank paints in terms of global governance, the alleviation of poverty, and the role of agriculture in relation to globalization. Although the Bank focuses less attention on the types of food rural farmers produce, its conception of the future of globalization illuminates a particular vision for rural farmers, laborers, and landless peoples. Working together with the WTO, the IMF, and UN food agencies, the Bank promotes a specific form of development that focuses on liberalization, privatization, free trade, technology, and good governance. While many of these strategies are not bad in and of themselves, the following chapters address some of the development strategies' advantages and disadvantages.

By renewing attention to small-scale farm productivity, the World Bank's 2008 Annual Report ostensibly makes a move in the right direction. However, it remains to be seen whether this "revolution" in small-scale productivity amounts to fundamental changes in the way the World Bank understands agriculture. Even if more attention is paid to the potential of small-scale farms, without recognizing that food and farming cannot be reduced to simple economic phenomena, food security will remain a problematic concept. If the ultimate goal of the World Bank and IMF is to integrate small-scale farmers into the global economy, food and agriculture will remain tied to a purely economic understanding of human relations. Although the World Bank plays a particularly influential role in how food and agriculture is conceived, the IMF, which serves as the financial arm of the global governance triad, must also be scrutinized in terms of its role in global governance and food security.

THE IMF

Of the three global governance institutions, the IMF is arguably the least concerned with agricultural development and food security. However, its function is still consequential for food security, and, as such, it must be understood in the larger context of global governance. The IMF outlines three foundational institutional objectives: surveillance, financial assistance, and technical assistance.[57] With a membership of 185 countries, the IMF oversees global economic stability by "monitoring the economic and financial polices" of member countries. Surveillance involves "expert assessment of economic and financial developments" in an effort to facilitate the exchange of goods and services, capital flow, and sustainable economic growth.[58] Financial assistance involves the processes by which countries can request economic assistance, in the form of loans, to regulate their specific macroeconomic climates. Loans are granted under "conditionalities" in which applicant countries must adhere to specific economic policy prescriptions coordinated by the consultant country and the IMF. Finally, the IMF provides technical assistance by offering countries advice on how to "effectively manage" economic policy and financial affairs.[59] Most of this assistance is offered to low and lower-middle income countries and involves a holistic approach that promotes policy strategies that bolster surveillance and financial assistance. In general, technical assistance focuses on "macroeconomic policy, tax policy and revenue administration, expenditure management, monetary policy, the exchange rate system, financial sector sustainability, and macroeconomic and financial statistics." Ultimately, technical assistance serves to diagnose, strategize, and implement financial policy that "aims to assist low-income countries [to] expand their participation in the global economy."[60]

While the IMF is not as influential with respect to food security as the WTO and World Bank, as a global institution dominated by the G7 countries, it exercises its influence through global financial governance. Poor and developing countries seeking IMF assistance must take certain steps to gain access to IMF funds, and the IMF subscribes to the World Bank and WTO model. Take for instance a press release from 2002:

Directors welcomed the opportunity to discuss the issue of market access for developing country exports, especially given the context of the multilateral trade negotiations in progress at the WTO. While the WTO provides the proper framework for these negotiations, the Fund, working closely with the World Bank and the WTO, has an important role to play in promoting and actively supporting trade liberalization among its members. This involves systematically raising the awareness of the benefits of free trade and of the costs imposed by market access restrictions in the context of the Fund's bilateral and multilateral surveillance activities, as well as policy advice and technical assistance in its areas of competence in support of countries' liberalization efforts, including on the timing and sequencing of liberalization, and on strategies to address the social and dislocation effects of trade reform. Directors underscored the complementarity between trade integration and financial integration, and the crucial importance of market access for the exports of developing countries to improve their prospects for durable growth and poverty reduction and ensure their successful integration in the globalized economy.[61]

As outlined above, the IMF focuses on developmental economic policies of free trade, liberalization, technical assistance, and financial integration as key determinants for reducing global poverty. With respect to agriculture specifically, the IMF's 2005 report "Doha Development Agenda and Aid for Trade" reiterated its commitment and support for trade strategies outlined by the continued efforts of the WTO Doha round. Focusing specifically on agricultural reform, the IMF suggests that the most successful strategies will remain focused on market access, domestic support, and export competition.

The IMF recommends three main objectives in terms of a "good" outcome for the original Doha round. First, "developed countries must adopt the same ambitious market openings in agriculture that they long ago adopted in manufacturers by eliminating export subsidies and substantially reducing applied tariffs and trade distorting domestic support; market access is particularly important." Second, "middle income countries, and poor countries more selectively, contribute with offers to open services markets, bring down high tariffs in manufacturers, and reduce barriers in heavily protected agricultural markets, while expressing a willingness to trade away 'special and differential treatment' for increased market access in agriculture and elsewhere to spur their own development." And finally, with respect to aid for trade, assistance from the international community should "help countries address supply side constraints to their participation in international markets and help to cope with transitional adjustment costs from liberalization."[62]

The IMF supports the same theoretical ground of global development and trade policy as the World Bank and the WTO. By coordinating with the Bank and the WTO, the Fund oversees financial aspects of governance, which in turn promote neoliberal policies of free trade, privatization, and deregulation. Although the Fund is not directly tied to issues of food security, it remains an important organization insofar as it also creates the financial conditions in which food security is achieved. The concept of food security as envisioned by organizations such as the UN, as well as the global conditions in which food security must operate, are further examined in the following chapter.

HISTORICAL ROOTS AND THE EMERGENCE OF FOOD SECURITY AND A GLOBAL FOOD REGIME

Thus far, the theories and strategies of global institutions such as the FAO, IFAD, WTO, World Bank, and IMF have been examined in an effort to demonstrate how international organizations conceive of agricultural development and food security. While these organizations offer a contemporary vision of how these topics should be guided in the future, it is important to recognize that the present status of development, agricultural reform, and food security did not emerge out of a vacuum; rather, these issues have evolved primarily over the course the 20th century. The following section offers a brief historical overview of major developments in the global food system.

According to Philip McMichael, one result of the new global economic order initiated by the creation of the World Bank and IMF was the restructuring of the global food industry. The "international food regime" that emerged in the postwar era centered on U.S.-directed production/distribution/consumption models.[63] After WWII, food economies emerged in the context of power relations between nation states, in which the food regime was partly an issue of "international relations of food, and partly about the world food economy."[64] In an effort to protect its agricultural markets, the United States, for example, adopted protective farm policies that included both import controls and export subsidies. Given the United States' economic and political power during the three decades following WWII, European and Third World economies increasingly had to model their agricultural policies along national and protectionist lines. However, at the same time, the free movement of capital during this period resulted in the integration of European and U.S. agri-food sectors. As such, the food regime that emerged between 1947 and 1972 was a tenuous combination of the "replication" of the U.S. model and the "integration" of European and U.S. agricultural sectors.[65] In other words, European states replicated the U.S. model by protecting certain goods in an effort to counter-balance U.S. protective measures, while other parts of the world—specifically the Third World—were forced to adapt their agricultural sectors to meet the demands of the evolving global food market.

One aspect of this evolution came with the inception of New Deal programs in the 1940s, whereby the United States sought to increase agricultural productivity through price supports of, and export subsidies to, farm products. This in turn motivated farmers to produce surplus reserves.

Surpluses mounted more persistently with the technological developments involved in industrialization of agriculture. Industrialization subordinated farms to emerging agro-food corporations, both as buyers of machines, chemicals, and animal feeds, and as sellers of raw materials to food manufacturing industries or livestock operations. Profits in the agro-food sector depended on the larger restructuring of the postwar economy toward mass production and mass consumption of animal products and high value-added manufactured foods, or what might be called 'durable foods.'[66]

One outcome of these policies was the emergence of agro-food corporations that sought to integrate European and U.S. agricultural markets. While both Europe and the United States continued with their protectionist policies, large corporations served as intermediaries between small and large scale farmers. Given the increased export of cheap grains by the United States and the increased demand for durable foods, Third World countries were forced to reorganize their agricultural sectors. This was especially important to the extent that corporations positioned themselves between "specialized livestock operations, which were their customers, and maize and soy farms, which sold to them."[67] Corporate demand for durable foods, which are made from generic ingredients such as sweeteners, fats, and starches, increased the possibilities for substitution, and as agro-food corporations became less dependent on traditional Third World products such as sugar cane and tropical oils (due to the possibility for substitution), these products became marginalized.[68] As such,

by the early 1970s, the food regime had caught the third world in a scissors. One blade was food import dependency. The other blade was declining revenues from traditional exports of tropical crops.[69]

For Third World countries, this scissor grip became all the more problematic as the world experienced a food crisis in 1973–74.

A massive grain deal between the Soviet Union and the United States resulted in the removal of large quantities of wheat, corn, and soy from the world market, which resulted in food prices tripling between 1972 and 1974. Coinciding with the food crisis, the global economy witnessed the infamous oil crisis in which oil prices also tripled. For Third World economies dependent on both food and oil, these duel crises intensified hardships. As a result, the option to borrow money from the United States (and other industrialized countries) became increasingly attractive. "Governing elites of these borrowing nations took the money as a way to avoid dealing with the deeper problems of solving their import dependence."[70]

This Third World borrowing culminated in the massive debt crisis of the 1980s. As least developed and developing countries fell further into debt, they were forced to seek out ways in which to manage their balance of payment deficits (which usually amounted to simply paying off the interest to loans made by industrial nations). As such, industrial nations, following the lead of the IMF and World Bank, initiated a massive program of debt management. From the standpoint of the Bretton Woods institutions this crisis was not a result of failed economic policy and management, but rather a failure on the part of Third World countries to adequately subscribe to industrialized models of economic integration.[71] As mentioned above, one of the main policy prescriptions was SAPs, which "demanded a restructuring of economic policy" with the "idea being that debtors should follow multilateral prescriptions for political and economic reforms to ensure economic growth and regular debt service."[72] Rather than address the deeper issues of poverty, the growing reliance on foreign goods, and massive debt, the IMF and World Bank continued to emphasize economic solutions to these problems. The following chapter takes a more in-depth look at the dilemmas this posed for least developed and developing nations

SUMMARY

The current concept of food security can be understood through the developmental theory and policy of global organizations such as IFAD and the FAO, as well as WTO trade arrangements and the World Bank's and IMF's poverty reduction strategies. One common theme that pervades all of these institutional strategies is the focus on alleviating poverty through developmental growth, with a specific focus on agricultural reform, trade, and technological progress. While these are indeed crucial issues given the fact that there are upwards of 840 million people experiencing hunger and malnutrition worldwide, the purpose of this investigation is to examine how the concept of food security is conceived within these matrices. While food security plays only one role in curbing global poverty and reducing hunger, the way it is conceived through theory and policy can illuminate broader perspectives on economic and cultural globalization.

UN organizations such as IFAD and the FAO view food security primarily in terms of how it contributes to alleviating poverty; however, food security as a goal of alleviating poverty can be distinguished from food security as an issue of developing rural economies and farming both to alleviate poverty and to sustain the cultural livelihoods of the rural poor. In this sense, food security is not only about ensuring that the world's hungry have enough to eat, but also about how food functions on a cultural and political level, namely as representative of the worldviews and lifestyles of the world's poor. As such, when we look at issues such as agricultural reform, trade, development and so forth, it is important to examine how different global governance institutions envision food security through these topics.

For example, scrutinizing IFAD and FAO policies on agricultural reform needs to take into account the intent and outcome of particular reform strategies and policies. If reform is considered in terms of poverty reduction, we need to ask if or how this may direct attention away from sustaining the cultural traditions of individual communities . One could examine this question through the lens of IFAD's understanding of knowledge management. In the context of working with the rural poor to craft successful growth and development strategies, IFAD nonetheless still functions in a managerial role. That is, IFAD reinforces the idea that current trends in global market integration require a managerial organization to help direct the assimilation of the rural poor into larger economic networks. Instead of engaging in a full critique of many globalization trends (such as trade, market integration, technological advances, etc.), IFAD chooses instead to work with these trends in a manner that is beneficial to the poor. While this is a valid strategy, we may also ask how this approach possibly silences voices that challenge the inevitability of current forms of economic and cultural globalization.

The inevitability of social and economic globalization is, arguably, most visible in the policy rhetoric and strategies of the WTO, World Bank, and IMF. While IFAD and the FAO are slightly more hesitant to subscribe to the idea that neoliberal and developmental economic theory is the panacea for curbing global poverty and achieving food security, the WTO, World Bank, and IMF argue that economic globalization holds the key to solving problems associated with global hunger and poverty. This is evidenced on a general level in WTO policies of trade liberalization, privatization, and trade management—with the underlying philosophy of competition, efficiency, and market fluidity—as guiding principles of a free economic market. On a specific level, food security falls within neoliberal and developmental paradigms expressed in the Doha trade negotiations. Agriculture in these discussions is, again, conceived in terms of how it fosters economic growth and can serve to alleviate poverty.

With the coordination of World Bank policies such as SAPs and IMF strategies of surveillance, financial, and technical assistance, we see how these three organizations are positioning themselves as global authorities of economic and cultural integration. By compelling least developed and developing nations to restructure their macroeconomic policies in accordance with neoliberal and developmental economic theory, these organizations recapitulate current trends in globalization, albeit with the rhetoric that past policy failures can be amended with greater coordination, political willpower, and sound economic policy strategies.[73]

The idea that there is one, inalienable path of globalization can be challenged by the historical, social and economic precursors to our current state of globalization. The strategies and policies of the WTO, World Bank, and IMF did not emerge unintentionally; rather, over the course of the 20th century, certain policy strategies created the conditions for our current state of affairs. For example, massive food surpluses, coupled with disastrous Third World debt, created ripe conditions for food aid programs, the foundation of current trade agreements, and SAPs. While organizations such as the WTO, World Bank, and IMF are hesitant to address the fundamental concept of global governance, this concept can be challenged. The following chapter addresses these issues through a critique of WTO, World Bank, and IMF policies, the concept of global governance itself, and the concept of food security as envisioned through agricultural reform and economic development.

CHAPTER 2

The Underside of Development

INTRODUCTION

In the first chapter we examined how food security is conceived by the World Bank and supported by policies of the WTO and IMF. UN organizations such as the FAO and IFAD advocate developmental models that focus on pro-poor economic growth through agricultural reform, sustainable development, and strengthening rural infrastructure. Alternatively, a more market-driven or neoliberal model is evident in the policies of the World Bank and IMF and in the trade arrangements of the WTO. Strategies of trade liberalization, deregulation, privatization, and the promotion of free-market economic integration are endorsed on the implicit notion that competition, efficiency, and profitability can be the impetus behind economic growth. Common to all of these institutions is the underlying assumption that economic growth is the guiding force behind achieving food security and eliminating global hunger and poverty.

Along these lines, one of the questions of this chapter is *to what end or purpose is developmental growth envisioned?* In addition to this question, it is also important to ask how food production, distribution, and consumption are envisioned in this process. What type of human relations does this notion of food security promote? These questions are addressed throughout this chapter and in the next, as the concept of food sovereignty presents an alternative to current conceptions of food security. Ultimately, the final two chapters demonstrate that multilateral organizations such as the World Bank, IMF, and WTO sustain a global economic order that supports a model of food security that is inadequate for curbing hunger and alleviating poverty.

As such, these organizations support a food security model that functions within a broader global governance framework that, arguably, constitutes a violation of human rights.

Moreover, concentrating on how we conceive of food within discourses on globalization and poverty provides an opportunity to question the problems of considering food simply as a commodity that can be produced, traded, and consumed like any other commodity in the market. How does the commodification of food explicitly or implicitly set the parameters of how we conceive of our world's natural resources? As discussed in chapter three, many food sovereignty advocates argue that the world's natural resources should not be viewed solely in terms of private ownership or how they serve the economic foundation of development and growth. Instead, these advocates argue that the world's natural resources were never owned in an economic sense in the first place, but rather are part of a natural environment whose cultural value supersedes its economic value. Conceiving of the world's resources as owned by all translates for many food sovereignty advocates into the claim that the right to food is a human right, a right that is founded upon the premise that our natural resources, and the cultivation of food thereby, are common to all humanity. As such, food security cannot be limited to the economic dimensions of global hunger and poverty. Instead, the cultural value of food production and consumption must play a central role in how we define food security. However, before investigating these issues, a critical analysis of food security as defined by the World Bank, IFAD, and FAO and supported by economic policies and trade arrangements of the IMF and WTO must be made to provide the context in which current conceptions of food security are critically challenged by the food sovereignty movement.

The next two sections investigate IFAD's and the FAO's developmental conceptions of globalization, which, while ostensibly focusing on pro-poor, developmental growth, remain founded on the notion of economic relationships directed by competition, efficiency, and the free market. Following this discussion, the policies of the World Bank, WTO, and IMF are challenged on the grounds that neoliberal economic theory and policy have proved largely detrimental to the world's poor. To bring this argument into focus, several case studies are incorporated to illustrate the failures of certain multilateral projects.

IFAD AND THE VISION FOR DEVELOPMENT AND POVERTY

As illustrated in chapter one, IFAD's Strategic Framework demonstrates how food security is inextricably tied to rural development. Food security will be achieved once the rural poor are enabled to take advantage of natural resource management, advances in agricultural technology, improved rural infrastructure, and competitive markets for agricultural inputs (i.e. produce). Policy strategies such as the implementation of microfinance institutions allow rural farmers and nonfarm workers to engage in free-market relationships in which competition, efficiency, and growth are encouraged. While IFAD recognizes that these developmental strategies need to be formulated with the participation of both IFAD policy coordinators and local communities, its strategy of knowledge management remains managerial in nature. As IFAD's document states, its organizational mission is to "learn systematically and collectively from its own projects and programs, and from the experience of its partners . . . deliver high quality services, and . . . to use the knowledge acquired to foster pro-poor policy reforms."[1] This sort of knowledge coordination is necessary given that rural farmers are not always privy to advances in agricultural technology, nor are they always aware of fluctuations in agricultural (and other) markets. Organizations such as IFAD are needed to help rural farmers acquire this knowledge. Criticizing the genuineness of IFAD's desire to help impoverished communities is somewhat unproductive. To a certain extent, IFAD is correct in identifying the causal link between achieving food security and the development of technology, knowledge of the global economic market, natural resources, and infrastructure. However, the role of these factors, as well as the way globalization is thereby conceived, marks only *one* way to conceive of food security.

IFAD's strategy of microfinance proves illuminating in determining to what end or purpose developmental growth is conceived. One of the central features of microfinance is the use of microcredit, whereby the poor can borrow funds to secure the financial base from which to generate capital. The hope is that these funds will be provided at a low interest rate to allow borrowers to repay their loans. The relationship between the borrower and the creditor is based on the classical economic assumption that creditors benefit from lending and debtors benefit from borrowing. Ideally, one of the central goals of borrowing microfunds is to enable people to invest in capital that will ultimately provide a steady source of income, which in turn will allow them to repay their initial loans and become self-sustainable.

Unfortunately, in some instances people use borrowed funds for purposes other than building a capital base or for entrepreneurial enterprises. The funds may be used for emergency purposes such as sending a child to school or paying for medical care.[2] These funds are still essential and desirable for people in dire need, but it is "also a sad reality that many microcredit loans help borrowers to survive or tread water more than they help them get ahead."[3] In sum, microfinance may serve to benefit some, but it should not be considered a panacea for curbing poverty or rapidly advancing development.

From an ethical perspective, one of the questions microfinance raises pertains to the type of human relations microfinance implicitly (and possibly explicitly) supports. For example, recalling IFAD's official policy stance, the organization recognizes how microfinance can be a double edged sword; namely, it can be successful in reducing poverty if orchestrated in a way the benefits both the borrower and the lender. However, IFAD falls short of questioning the nuances of profit motivation. It views microfinance in traditional economic terms in which successful growth depends on competition, efficiency, and self-interest. "Microfinance is not a charity," and assistance should only be extended to "those MFIs that have demonstrated their capacity for resource mobilization, cost coverage, profitability, and dynamic growth."[4] While ensuring the integrity of the borrower/lender relationship is vital for microfinance to succeed, this pragmatic aspect begs the question of how microfinance may serve to impose a form of human relations that is driven essentially by competition, efficiency, and profitability.

For example, in India, the microfinance organization Grameen created a partnership with the Monsanto Company in 1998. This partnership ultimately served the interests of Monsanto as it created markets for Monsanto products. Instead of promoting rural farmer knowledge, conservation of natural resources, and the sustainability of farmer livelihoods, this partnership simply created markets in which cheap Monsanto products could be sold to Indian farmers. Microfinance credit that was extended to farmers was spent on Monsanto's expensive herbicides, seed, royalties and, technology fees.[5] While Monsanto can argue that its seeds and produce increase food security through more efficient production, increased yields, and advanced agricultural technologies, it does not address how, on the one hand, its influence alters traditional agricultural practices, and on the other, how microfinance potentially dismantles traditional farmer livelihoods. For example, if credit is extended to purchase nonrenewable seeds (i.e. genetically modified seeds that yield one crop generation and must be purchased with each crop cycle) instead of farmer-saved seeds, farmers become increasingly indentured to corporate monopolization.[6] In certain contexts microfinance creates dependence on market mechanisms.

It is important to highlight the ethical implications of these types of strategies. Despite the focus on building rural and impoverished economies, policies such as microfinance illustrate the underside of certain conceptions of developmental growth. The idea that competition, efficiency, and profitability are the underlying forces behind developmental growth demonstrates "the deepening capitalist order entering every sphere of life."[7] The food sovereignty movement examined in the following chapter illustrates that many people are not motivated solely by economic factors. Instead, for example, the lives of rural farmers are centered on the cultural traditions associated with harvesting traditional foods and resources, consuming healthy and culturally significant foods, and building and sustaining local communities based on local values, beliefs, and traditions.

THE FAO AND AGRICULTURAL REFORM

Although the FAO's role as a development agency differs slightly from that of IFAD, its vision of food security is similar. The FAO defines food security as the access for all people at all times to enough food for an active, healthy life. The three key ideas underlying this definition are: the adequacy of food availability (effective supply); the adequacy of food access, i.e. the ability of the individual to acquire sufficient food (effective demand); and the reliability of both. Food security can, therefore, be a failure of availability, access, reliability or some combination of these factors. Inherent in this modern concept of food security is an understanding of food producers and consumers as *economic agents* (my emphasis).[8]

This definition reveals the FAO's fundamental, economic conception of food security. When it comes to food security we must look at humans as economic agents, people governed in terms of economic relations. Implicit in this understanding of food security is the idea that humans are autonomous, rational beings who interact through competition rather than cooperation, self-interest rather than community, and consumerism rather than culturally sustainable relations.[9] Food security, then, must be conceived on a theoretical level in terms of this economic framework of human relations. According to the FAO definition, food security will be accomplished through effective supply and demand economic theory, whereby people need to produce enough food to supply the market and enough resources to purchase food on the market. Agricultural development is also a central concern of the FAO, and an examination of its policies further demonstrates this vision of globalization and human relations.

As the FAO's "The State of Food Insecurity in the World" document recommends, given that 70 percent of the global population still pursues agrarian livelihoods, it is imperative that growth in the agricultural sector be the driving force behind economic development and food security. According to the FAO's current twin track approach, long term policy strategies must enhance the productive potential of rural areas in order to provide capital and financial stability for the rural poor. In addition, short term policies and programs are required to make the transition into larger, global agricultural markets as smooth as possible. More specifically, "the first track calls for increased investment in agriculture and rural areas in order to improve productivity and build competitiveness," while the second track "calls for safety nets to protect vulnerable groups from trade-related shocks and to allow the poor to take advantage of the economic opportunities arising from trade."[10]

While this approach acknowledges that free trade can be a double-edged sword; namely, beneficial to the poor as long as trade works in their favor, it also further underscores the economic rationale behind policy formulation. Food security can be accomplished through increased agricultural productivity, which in turn allows rural farmers to produce crops that are competitive in the global market. Increasing production of staple goods will allow farmers to be competitive in local economies, while increasing production of foods that give these communities a comparative advantage will allow them to be competitive in global markets.

Both the FAO and WTO agree that this strategy will work only if trade-distorting subsidies are curbed or eliminated. Reducing agricultural subsidies enables farmers to produce food goods that are competitive in both local and global markets because these goods can be bought and sold according to world market prices, which are not manipulated by protectionist policies that distort price levels. While the FAO urges, first, for the production of goods for local economies, its ultimate goal is to enable farmers to compete in global markets. However, the belief that competition is the driving force behind production reinforces the idea that farmers should be concerned more with how to produce for the global economy than for the local community. Although the FAO claims that small-scale agriculture is the most efficient means to curbing poverty and achieving food security, the emphasized rationale behind this strategy is economic rather than cultural. Namely, the FAO recognizes that rural farmers' livelihoods are often centered on farming, but if poverty reduction rather than community development is the end goal, economic stabilization and productivity must take center stage.

The FAO's strategy for reducing global hunger emphasizes the role of both multilateral institutions and national governments. As outlined in the FAO's policy proposals, not only do multinational organizations need to play a role in poverty reduction and agricultural growth, but national governments need to exercise the political willpower to help the poor. While this vision is important to the extent that it emphasizes the role of national governments in implementing successful policies, it does not adequately highlight how national governments are increasingly bound by policies of multilateral organizations such as the IMF, World Bank, and WTO. If agricultural growth is accomplished through agricultural reform that disenfranchises rural farmers, political willpower is truncated because governments are compelled to craft macroeconomic policies that are often disadvantageous to the poor. Problems associated with World Bank, IMF, and WTO polices are examined in the case study of Mexico below, but it is worth highlighting a central conflict here. From a developmental perspective, the FAO and IFAD promote pro-poor growth, which is good on a rhetorical level, but insufficient if not implemented in practice. With respect to the World Bank, its 2008 report on agricultural development represents a shift in emphasis to the role of small-scale agricultural productivity. However, as outlined in chapter one, this small-scale revolution is still conceived in terms of neoliberal economic ideas of efficiency, competition, and profitability.

Furthermore, these approaches betray a conception of food as a typical commodity. If food is considered simply as a commodity, it should be traded like any other good in the market. Namely, the production of food should be conceived in terms of its economic value. While people need enough food to be healthy and active, the FAO makes little to no reference to the cultural value of food. A healthy and active life can come from a sufficient caloric intake, but a *culturally significant life* requires a more nuanced definition of food production and consumption. If food is conceived of as a standard, tradable commodity, consumption becomes an inflexible variable in the production, distribution, consumption cycle.

THE UNITED STATES AND FOOD SECURITY

The distinction between the neoliberal economic approach of the IMF, World Bank, and WTO and the developmental approach of IFAD and the FAO is further complicated when we look at the role of powerful nations such as the United States. As former UN Special Rapporteur Jean Zigler noted,

there are profound internal contradictions in the United Nations system. On the one hand, the UN agencies emphasize social justice and human rights . . . On the other hand, the Bretton Woods institutions [the World Bank and the IMF], along with the government of the United States of America and the World Trade Organization, oppose in their practice the right to food . . . emphasizing liberalization, deregulation, privatization and the compression of state domestic budgets—a model which in many cases produces greater inequalities.[11]

These contradictions were clearly demonstrated in the 2002 World Food Summit in Rome. During this meeting, the United States refused to sign an international Right to Food text that defined food as a human right. Ultimately, U.S. negotiators prevailed and the final text contained only vague references as what constituted a human right to food, as well as the United States's obligation to enforce this right. The following chapters take a closer look at the problems associated with conceiving of food security simply in terms of international human rights, but the U.S. position on how food security specifically (and the reduction of poverty generally) should be conceived is worth mentioning here. The Bush administration's final statement regarding the summit is illuminating:

The United States believes . . . that the issue of adequate food can only be viewed in the context of the right to a standard of living adequate for health and well-being as set forth in the Universal Declaration of Human Rights [UDHR], which includes the opportunity to secure food, clothing, housing, medical care and necessary social services. *Further, the United States believes that the attainment of the right to an adequate standard of living is a goal or aspiration to be realized progressively that does not give rise to any international obligation or any domestic legal entitlement and it does not diminish the responsibilities of national governments towards their citizens . . . Additionally, the United States understands the right of access to food to mean the opportunity to secure food and not a guaranteed entitlement* (my emphasis).[12]

The wording of this statement demonstrates a particularly ideological definition of food security. Food security should not be premised on an international human right to food; rather, local governments have the primary responsibility to provide for their citizens. As such, state governments, and the U.S. government specifically, should not be obligated by an internationally binding agreement to provide food security for the rest of the world. The closest the United States comes to advocating a right to food is through abstract language of "the right of access to food," and the "opportunity to secure food." In other words, food is not a guaranteed entitlement.

Phrasing commitments to a human right to food in such a way has two implications. On the one hand, countries such as the United States are not legally bound to provide food to those in need. In effect, this makes universal human rights declarations meaningless. Wealthy countries can pay lip service to a general declaration of human rights without specifying the concomitant responsibilities and obligations that emerge from such commitments. On the other hand, by directing attention to the role of individual governments, the United States and multilateral organizations such as the IMF, World Bank, and WTO are unencumbered in promoting policies that focus on economic solutions to poverty and food security. While these themes are addressed in the following chapters, it is worth mentioning up front that the U.S. statement on food security is representative of a broader ideological narrative that concentrates on the economic rather than the cultural face of globalization.

For instance, by focusing on the economic aspects of growth, the United States' stance suggests that poverty is a result of an unwillingness to or an incapability of countries or individuals to produce. Instead, the world's poor need the *opportunity*, rather than the entitlement, to become self-sufficient. This shifts attention away from the types of policies that are implemented toward the *ability* of governments and their poor to successfully assimilate to these policies. As such, neoliberal policies of trade liberalization, privatization, and deregulation are not the problem; rather, it is the unwillingness or refusal of governments and their people to ascribe to these policies that is the primary obstacle for achieving food security. This, of course, is an ideological position that supports neoliberal economic policies of growth and development and denigrates alternative conceptions of globalization and food security.

FOREIGN AID, FOOD AID, AND THE POLITICS OF U.S. FOOD SECURITY

Food aid is part and parcel of larger foreign aid programs that assist developing and least developed countries by providing money, technology, food, and so forth. As briefly mentioned in chapter one, food aid programs were initially implemented by the United States as a means to simultaneously discharge food surpluses and provide food to the global poor. For example, in the 1950s, the United States Agency for International Development (USAID) implemented its Food for Peace program, which on a rhetorical level seemed laudable, but in reality proved problematic for many aid recipient countries. As the United States dumped surpluses of wheat into Third World markets, not only did recipient, domestic food market prices plummet, but dependency on U.S. wheat intensified. For example, by 1986, 7 of the 10 leading importers of U.S. farm goods were previous Food for Peace recipients.[13] Not only have we seen the problems associated with dumping surpluses into Third World markets and the intensification of food dependency, but the actual management of food aid has proven inadequate in many instances.

For food aid to be most effective, it should arrive prior to the harvest period so as to have minimal effects on local food prices as well as curb hunger resulting from previously poor harvests. The Food for Peace program had particularly devastating effects on Somalia in 1985–86, for example, when food aid arrived during the annual harvest period and depressed local prices and discouraged local farmers to produce at optimum levels (due to the fact that they could not generate as much income because of U.S. imports). This became especially poignant as certain regions of Somalia were struck by famine a few months later. As a result of dumped goods and the disincentive for local farmers to produce at optimal levels, when food was needed it did not reach famine stricken areas, and thousands of people died unnecessarily.

Aside from organizations such as USAID, the UN and multilateral organizations such as the IMF and World Bank also have an influential role in determining the form aid should take, which countries deserve aid, and the political conditions under which aid will be successful or unsuccessful. Critiques of current forms of food aid center around the idea that increased food aid is the panacea for food insecurity. Perennial problems associated with food aid programs include the conditions under which governments are required to (re)structure their macroeconomic policies to be eligible to receive food aid; whether the distribution of food aid reduces poverty for rural farmers and landless peoples or disproportionately benefits landed elites; and whether food aid creates unfavorable conditions of food dependency.[14]

Setting aside the issue of wealthy nations' responsibility to provide funds for food aid—noting that the United States ranks poorly in relation to many other wealthy countries—food aid policies can also be investigated in terms of how they propagate a certain vision of economic globalization. One notable problem with food aid stems from the fact that it is often tied to structural adjustment and conditionalities imposed by the World Bank and IMF. Generally, this process can be summed up as follows:

Conditionality works by 'tranching' economic assistance packages—that is, dividing the total sum to be donated or loaned to a recipient country into a series of smaller disbursements to be made over time, called tranches. Before each disbursement is made, the recipient must make policy changes spelled out in the 'covenants' of the aid agreement that they must sign with USAID.[15]

These covenants can be any number of structural adjustment requirements that governments must complete before disbursements are made. As we have already seen, these structural adjustment policies proved disastrous for many

Third World countries during the 1980s and 1990s. Food aid policies instituted during this period were based on failed World Bank and IMF strategies for debt reduction, privatization, trade liberalization, and so forth. This resulted in a paradoxical situation in which, on the one hand, the policies instituted by multilaterals increased income inequality and devastated rural farmers by flooding local markets with food below the cost of local production, and, on the other hand, ensured that these people became dependent on the food provided through aid programs. Regardless of the form of the aid program initiated (i.e. food for work, health, education, and now oil), the end result is the same for rural farmers and peasants. Foreign food enters the economy, distorts local food markets, and drives farmers off their land because they can no longer compete with depressed food prices. Ultimately, this results in food dependency as rural farmers are forced to leave their land—and often migrate to urban areas in search of wage labor.

As is also addressed in this chapter, one strategy and result of World Bank and IMF economic assistance is the influx of foreign investment, mainly in developing countries. The major players in foreign investment are transnational corporations, which, with respect to agribusiness, have wreaked havoc on many local economies. In the food sector, these corporations are generally free to enter local economies and implement Green Revolution style reforms. By introducing chemical-intensive crops, genetically modified seeds, and expensive capital inputs, these corporations continue the destruction of local farmer livelihoods. While it might seem a stretch to link transnational corporations (TNCs) to food aid programs, the problem lies in the general conception of food insecurity by multilaterals such as the World Bank and IMF. If the problem is conceived in simple terms of needing to deliver more food to suffering people—and the solution to this problem lies initially with structural adjustment in the hopes of generating growth—then foreign investment, as an aspect of this growth, should be encouraged. In the agricultural sector, if agribusinesses are considered as vehicles for generating growth, then TNCs can certainly play an integral role in food aid, or so it is claimed.

Alongside these structural problems of food aid, there are also problems associated with corruption and waste. Reports abound of how foreign aid funds (whether in the form of food, financial, or developmental project aid) never reach their target audience. Often aid money is used by aid workers or elite intermediaries in recipient countries to pay for the lavish homes, social clubs, parties, vehicles, and so forth.[16]

Waste is also a problematic issue with respect to aid groups. For example, during the great famine of 1979 in Kampuchea (Cambodia), the private voluntary organization Food for Hunger arranged a shipment of survival food and drugs that was so old that "San Francisco zoo-keepers had stopped feeding it to their animals and some of the drugs had expired fifteen years earlier." In another instance, during an African crisis a British charity sent "packs of tea, tissues and Tampax, while a West German voluntary agency sent 1,000 polystyrene igloos, which proved too hot for the intended recipients" and thus had to be burned. Or, finally, take the example in which a European aid agency delivered 15,000 tons of maize to Mozambique, which upon arrival was found to be so full of broken grains, impurities, and mold it was completely unfit for human consumption.[17] These are just a few of many examples of how aid agencies often fail to deliver the proper relief goods to impoverished or famine stricken victims.

In part, these types of waste problems can be attributed to the sheer number of aid organizations we have today. For example, there are at least 16 United Nations agencies involved in disaster relief.[18] These agencies often have specialized areas of concern (for example, medical treatment or food shortages), and this often translates to competition over what they believe needs to be done to solve particular problems. The problem here is one of coordination. If aid agencies cannot concretely determine what needs to be done, lives may be lost.

Part of the problem with these types of bureaucratic inefficiencies involves who is in charge of aid projects. Often famine, refugee, or food relief efforts are coordinated by foreign individuals who do not understand the nature of particular problems. Given that most aid workers are temporary, it is often difficult for them to get a thorough understanding of both the needs of impoverished communities and political circumstances that may complicate the distribution of aid. This is not to suggest that all foreign aid workers should abandon the aid effort, but to point out that they are often caught up in larger structural problems that incapacitate their projects.

Foreign aid should not be abolished, yet the problems associated with how and who governs aid programs require critical evaluation of the intent and effectiveness of aid and charity organizations. If multilateral organizations exercise harmful influence on how and when aid is dispersed, if food aid proves detrimental to local farmers and economies, and if corruption and waste result in deaths that could have otherwise been prevented, then the idea and practice of foreign aid deserve reevaluation.

THE WTO AND TRADE

As outlined in chapter one, the WTO plays an influential role in the way global trade arrangements influence the effort to achieve food security. The WTO endorses trade arrangements based on trade liberalization, market access, and privatization of state services. With respect to food and agriculture, the WTO concentrates on market access to food products, and in the Agreement on Agriculture in 1995, introduced measures to curb export subsidies and domestic support with the belief that reducing trade barriers would allow for an unfettered flow of agricultural goods. While the WTO recognizes the risks inherent to trade liberalization—namely that structural adjustment policies will inevitably include economic and social lags that require macroeconomic management in the form of social safety nets, gradual reduction of export subsidies, and domestic support—it argues that some sacrifice is necessary because a free market will ultimately alleviate global poverty and provide food security. The following section takes a closer look at the WTO's strategies and investigates the actual record of their successes.

The WTO's role in agriculture and food security did not emerge out of a vacuum; rather, it materialized on the shoulders of global governance strategies stemming back to the middle of the 20th century. As we saw in the last chapter, beginning in the 1970s, the United States and Europe experienced a food crisis in which massive surpluses of food could not be absorbed by domestic markets.[19] To alleviate domestic food crises, the United States and Europe sought new, Third World or Southern markets to export their food surpluses. The oil crisis in the early 1970s forced many Third World countries, which were dependent on Northern oil and food, to take out massive loans to mitigate economic downturns. Widespread loan distributions culminated in the massive Third World debt crisis of the early 1980s and set the stage for a reconfiguration of global economic and trade networks. As discussed in the first chapter, one solution to these crises came in the form of SAPs encouraged by the World Bank. Among other things, SAPs instituted general trade liberalization policies that asymmetrically opened up Southern economies. As such, Southern agricultural movements, as well as many governments, complained that these trade arrangements were unfairly biased toward U.S. (and industrialized countries) interests.

Food rights activists often center their complaints on domestic price supports, export subsidies, and dumping. These are complex issues that deserve attention given that critics of the WTO attempt to unravel the benefits and harms of these mechanisms. Domestic subsidies are "government payments and services to farmers and agribusinesses" that help boost the agricultural sector. The WTO divides these subsidies into price-distorting and non-price-distorting subsidies. Price-distorting subsidies, for example, are payments and services rendered to farmers and agribusinesses who produce goods destined for export. If these particular products would not be produced without the aid of subsidies, they are considered trade-distorting because free market competition would result in other providers supplying these particular goods at a lower market price. Although the United States and Europe have ostensibly sanctioned the reduction of subsidies, Southern governments contend that, de facto, this is not enforced. The issue for Southern governments is not necessarily the elimination of all forms of subsidies, but rather a more egalitarian subsidy regime. These governments differentiate between wasteful subsidies and those that help maintain "legitimate environmental, economic, and rural development purposes."[20] Unfortunately, many WTO programs conjoin these beneficial subsidies with trade-distorting subsidies and thus call for their elimination *tout court*. Export subsidies are also a central issue of debate. These subsidies are mainly provided to large agribusinesses and are considered heavily trade-distorting insofar as these large firms can export extremely low-priced goods in massive quantity. While the United States and Europe have agreed to slash these forms of subsidies, many trading partners are skeptical of whether this will in fact happen. Finally, the main problem with domestic and export subsidies involves the issue of dumping. Generally speaking, dumping refers to the export of products below the cost of production (with nuanced discussion regarding whether one is looking at domestic or global cost of production). When foreign goods enter domestic markets at prices lower than the cost of production, the recipient country's farmers (or producers) are unable to compete with the price of these goods. Dumping is a complex issue given that it is usually most damaging to small-scale farmers who produce primarily for domestic markets. However, dumping is, at times, not of central concern for recipient country governments who cater to larger, wealthier farmers. To this extent, the debate around export subsidies includes a variety of actors, including small-scale rural farmers and peasants; wealthy, elite farmers; national governments; and the WTO. Despite these numerous actors, rural farmers and peasants incur the harmful brunt of subsidies that result in dumping.

Alongside the issues of domestic subsidies, supports, and export subsidies, the WTO has also drawn heated condemnation for its sponsorship of the TRIPS and TRIMS agreements. The WTO contends that the TRIPS agreement will provide countries with the capacity to bring complaints to the international community as well as a standardized and egalitarian platform from which to settle trade disputes. Ideally, the TRIPS agreement will protect domestic corporate innovations from being hijacked by other countries. In reality, however, many farmer and food rights activists argue the TRIPS agreement unfairly benefits agribusiness, opens the door for corporations to engage in harmful ecological practices, and infringes upon farming practices and traditions that have been around for millennia.

For example, the TRIPS agreement outlines the rules governing patents, copyrights, and trademarks. These guidelines are also extended to "living resources," including "genes, cells, seeds, plants and animals," which can now be patented and "owned" as intellectual property.[21] The composition of the TRIPS agreement during the Uruguay round was crafted in part by U.S. corporations, including agribusiness giants such as Monsanto.[22] The controversy that still surrounds the patenting of living resources centers around the idea that living organisms and biodiversity, which are self-creating, can somehow be "defined as machines and artifacts made and invented by the patentee."[23] For example, rural farmers have been saving their most productive and genetically successful seeds for centuries. Under the TRIPS guidelines, many of these practices are deemed illegal insofar as they infringe on patent rights.

Furthermore, as a result of the TRIPS agreement, giant biotechnology and chemical companies have emerged at an alarming rate. Currently, the top 10 seed companies control upwards of one-third of the commercial seed market. Forty percent of U.S. vegetable seeds come from a single source, and the top five vegetable seed companies control 75 percent of the global vegetable seed market. Companies such as DuPont and Monsanto together control 73 percent of the U.S. seed corn market. With respect to the commercial soybean market, only four companies (Monsanto, DuPont, Syngenta, Dow) control at least 47 percent of the market. Finally, at the end of 1998, a single company, Mississippi-based Delta & Pine Land, controlled more than 70 percent of the U.S. cottonseed market. Delta & Pine Land is perhaps best known for its notorious patent on genetic seed sterilization.[24] These are just a few of the astonishing figures representative of the increasing monopolization of certain agricultural sectors and products.

Given these alarming consolidations, the TRIPS agreement essentially affords giant corporations the ownership of traditional farming techniques, indigenous and traditional knowledge, and, ultimately, living organisms. The increasing influence of these corporate giants is further evidence of the failures of WTO trade liberalization policies to successfully improve the plight of the poor, and consequently achieve food security.

Alongside the failures of trade liberalization, WTO privatization recommendations have also proved detrimental to many developing countries' economies. While privatization strategies can occasionally prove beneficial to national economies if implemented within certain political, economic, and social circumstances, many of these policies create increased inequality in terms of income and asset distribution, especially in transitional countries such as Latin America.[25] As shown in the case study, "Mexico, Structural Adjustment, and Food," privatization often results in the consolidation of power and wealth in the hands of a few corporations or sectors, leading to conditions of wealth concentration similar to those outlined above. In the agricultural sector, privatization often results in the consolidation of small-scale farms into larger farms that produce one crop for mass production and distribution. The argument for small-scale farming is expanded upon in the following chapter, but it is worth noting that small-scale agriculture, contrary to popular (and some scientific) belief, can be more efficient in terms of environmental conservation, produce greater yields, and allow for greater diversity in crop production. Privatization policies in the agricultural sector often serve to dismantle small-farm networks and intensify the use of heavy machinery, harmful chemicals, and expensive capital inputs. The following section addresses this issue insofar as it is tied to the agricultural reform policies of the World Bank.

THE WORLD BANK AND MARKET LED AGRARIAN REFORM

As outlined in chapter one, the World Bank's influence on food security comes in large part through its broader institutional goals of providing technological and financial assistance to developing (and least developed) countries. While development assistance differs according to region, country, and type, the Bank subscribes to the general belief that food security

will be achieved through macroeconomic stabilization policies that encourage privatization, trade liberalization, and deregulation. Although the
Bank has recently shifted strategies away from international governance of
economic policy to more state-level coordinated strategies, it is still important to examine its historical record to understand the current status of
food security.[26] Despite the fact that the Bank has begun to critically examine the effectiveness of particular SAPs, this section begins with a critical
examination of some of the Bank's failed policies.

Recalling the policy strategies outlined in "Reaching the Rural Poor," the
World Bank's SAPs recommended "a focus on crop and livestock yields to
market demands and incomes," from "staples to high value crops," and from
"primary production to the entire food chain."[27] Initially, the World Bank's
general SAP strategies focused on purely market-driven agricultural reform,
which emphasized production as a means to increase surpluses destined
for export and trade. However, the Bank's 2008 report on development and
agriculture shifted this emphasis slightly toward a "productivity revolution
in small-holder farming." This is a shift in focus away from production for
output sake toward production for boosting local economies. However, the
Bank's underlying economic philosophy remains the same. Agricultural reform can contribute to alleviating poverty and hunger because it is an economic activity that generates income. This focus on the economic functions
of agriculture reduces farmer livelihoods to purely economic terms and
remains vulnerable to market led agricultural reform.

Raj Patel outlines the general theory of market-led agrarian reform promoted by the World Bank. Generally speaking, market-led reform is a "ho-
mogenous series of policies that form a sequence" in which reform begins
with mapping and surveying common or public lands. Once these common
or public parcels of land are mapped and surveyed, state governments usually attempt to install land titling regimes, whereby the land in question is
considered privatized. The titling of lands allows markets to facilitate the
distribution of these lands and credit institutions to fund the transfers. Once
the lands are distributed, governments fund the production schemes of the
beneficiaries of these lands. In other words, the final goal of the process is
the "complete private ownership of land, and functioning land markets in
which land . . . is bought, sold, and rented like any other commodity."[28]

The debate over the most efficient, productive, and beneficial process
of land reform generally falls between strategies of market-led reform and
conventional, usually state-led reform.[29] From a pro-market perspective, rural poverty can be attributed to the fact that poor farmers do not have clear
or secure private property rights. Without clear and secure private property rights, banks and other financial institutions are wary to invest in rural
economies. The most desirable framework for reform would be one in which
underused or common lands are privatized, which in turn allows investors and financial institutions to decide which producers are most competitive in local and global markets. Essentially, privatization establishes an

environment in which the most efficient and productive farms will survive. The Bank agrees, arguing, "It has long been recognized that a framework of secure, transparent and enforceable property rights has been the precondition for investment and economic growth."[30]

However, critics of market-led reform take issue with the type of reform policies implemented. The problem with a market-based approach is not so much the idea of securing private property rights. In fact, securing property is often a prerequisite for rural growth and food security. Instead, farmers take issue with World Bank reforms that primarily seek to (re)distribute land to the most efficient farmers. This leads to land concentration in larger, wealthier farms, which often produce for export rather than local consumption.

The promarket notion of taking in only the fittest beneficiaries—i.e. the most economically efficient and financially competitive peasants—is diametrically opposed to the fundamental notion of redistributive land reform, which has been conceptualized precisely because the need to create a class of efficient and competitive peasants (and/or rural proletariat), one requirement of which is the control over land resources by the actual tillers and workers . . . Such property-based deprivation breeds disadvantages, such as social exclusion, political disempowerment, and a lack of formal education, all of which contribute to and perpetuate economic inefficiency and financial noncompetitiveness.[31]

Recalling the driving question in this chapter—to what end or purpose developmental growth is envisioned—market-led agricultural reform is characteristic of a reductionist approach to food security specifically and global poverty in general. The purpose of market-led land reform is to establish land ownership for the most efficient economic producers. The end goal of this type of reform involves creating farms that can produce a commodity—namely whatever crop has a comparative advantage in the global economy—destined for trade and export.

The underlying premise of World Bank economic and trade management is the idea that growth is the engine behind curbing poverty. However, as our investigation of SAPs has demonstrated, economic growth in terms of policies such as market-led agricultural reform often proves detrimental to rural and peasant farmers. Critics of the World Bank also identify a deeper problem with the Bank's economic management. Setting aside for the moment the failures of structural adjustment, another way to examine the policies of the World Bank is to query whether these organizations actually craft strategies and policies that improve growth.[32] Even if the Bank pursues macroeconomic growth policies that detrimentally affect rural and peasant farmers in favor of policies that decrease overall poverty rates, their record is still ambiguous. The following case study examines whether the Bank's policies resulted in macroeconomic growth with respect to Mexico, as well as offers another example of how macroeconomic management has had damaging effects on the tortilla industry, one of Mexico's most culturally valued industries.

CASE STUDY: MEXICO, STRUCTURAL ADJUSTMENT, AND FOOD

From many multilateral institutional estimates, Mexico represents the model reformer with respect to SAPs.[33] Walden Bello notes that Mexico's initial motivation behind agreeing to structural adjustment policies of the World Bank and IMF was to reduce its debt. However, despite the initial framework of the 1989 World Bank and IMF-sponsored plan for adjustment, Mexico never really achieved debt reduction; rather, it achieved debt rescheduling. By 1991, Mexico's debt was $3 billion more than when the SAPs were originally implemented. Following the 1998 election, the government of Carlos Salinas de Gortari continued, albeit at a more rapid pace, efforts to modernize the Mexican economy through neoliberal economic policies such as the privatization of state agencies.[34]

The theory behind the World Bank and IMF adjustment was that the elimination of market distorting, government guided economic interventions would increase growth and make Mexico a more market friendly nation. Through a series of policies including wage restraints, devaluation of the currency (peso), and liberalizing foreign trade, the World Bank and IMF believed that Mexico could service its debt payments through increased export revenue. A series of currency devaluations, however, had a counterproductive effect as "increased exports from Mexico actually contributed to lowering their price in world markets, so that the value of Mexico's exports was actually less in 1988 than it had been in 1982."[35] As a result, the massive amount of financial resources exiting the country (7–11% of GDP) left Mexico with a per capita GDP comparable to its levels in the 1970s. Trade liberalization policies also had counterproductive effects. As import tariffs were lowered and import licenses eliminated, bankruptcies closed down hundreds of factories. For example, the domestic textile and clothing industry alone shrunk by 5 percent in 1992. This had drastic social ramifications as real wages decreased by 41 percent between 1982 and 1988. As a result, the unemployment rate rose to 20 percent and the under-employment rate rose to 40 percent, which had the effect of driving "half the population below the poverty line."[36]

Despite these consequences, Mexico continued its structural adjustment programs into the 1990s. Privatization increased and the number of state-owned industries decreased substantially. National banks were transferred into private hands and the Mexican government loosened its foreign investment regulations in an effort to encourage foreign investment. As a result, foreign investment rose from U.S. $2.6 million in 1900 to U.S. $4.6 million in 1991. Despite this inflow of foreign investment, structural adjustment damaged the economy, and by 1992 GDP growth decelerated and Mexico's debt had increased dramatically. The 1982 national account deficit of U.S. $4 billion had risen to U.S. $20 billion by 1992, due in large part to demand for imported goods that were previously managed by national industries. By reducing protection for local industries and increasing dependence on foreign goods, structural adjustment resulted in Mexico losing its ability to be self-sustainable in terms of growth. Not only did structural adjustment have macro-level consequences, local and community industry was damaged as well.

These political and economic developments had an influence on maize, one of Mexico's millennia-old traditional food goods that is used to make tortillas. Dating back to ancient Aztec traditions, the tortilla has held sacred and cultural value for Mexican peoples. The "social life" of the tortilla that has evolved over the last century illustrates the cultural ramifications of certain IMF, World Bank, and WTO policies. By the 1960s, when technological advances allowed for mass production of the tortilla, the Mexican food system was moving toward a path of self-sustainability.[37] Part of the Mexican government's effort to increase maize and tortilla production was to provide food security for both the rural and urban poor as well as integrate the *campesinos* (rural farmers) into a protected domestic market of indigenous food production.

By reaffirming the cultural importance of the tortilla, the Mexican government simultaneously improved food security and established this particular food as one aspect of economic and national identity.

The government's strategies for meeting the welfare needs of the people were linked to the people's staple food, the tortilla. Maize and tortillas circulated in protected markets, reinforcing the cultural criteria that viewed the tortilla as somehow incommensurable and incapable of being subjected to an unregulated free market economy.[38]

By the 1970s, however, the social life of the tortilla began to evolve as corporate and government production of tortilla flour surpassed historical records. Traditionally, the tortilla was made from hand-pressed wet maize (dough). However, with the mass production of flour, tortilla production today largely begins with a dry, flour base. As one analyst remarks, "In this sense we can speak, materially, of the shift to dry flour as the desiccation or drying out of the maize dough, and perhaps, symbolically, we might speak of the desecration of the tortilla culture."[39]

This transition from traditional maize tortillas to flour tortillas was also influenced by Roberto Gonzalez Barrera, a prominent businessman who became known as the King of Tortillas. A close ally of president Salinas, Barrera used his governmental connections to amass Maseca, one of the most lucrative tortilla businesses in Mexico.[40] To keep the price of tortillas low, in the late 1980s the Mexican government pumped millions of dollars in subsidies into corn production. However, these subsidies highly favored Maseca, and in 1994 the business had received $300 million in subsidies, which constituted 43 percent of Maseca's net revenues.[41] Not only did this monopolization process exemplify cronyism at its worst, it also contributed to the destruction of many *tortillerias* (small tortilla vendors).

This evolution of tortilla production is inextricable from the context of social and economic globalization, and specifically the policies of the IMF and World Bank. The structural adjustment programs Mexico was compelled to initiate due to defaulting on loans in 1982 resulted, in part, in the privatization of public agencies and the reduction of subsidies to farmers. The culmination of this process with the inception of the North American Free Trade Agreement (NAFTA) resulted in the reunion of corn and maize in global markets, whereby cheap U.S. corn flooded Mexico, "driving small farmers, millers, and *tortillerias* out of production, pushing them off their land and out of a livelihood."[42] It is also interesting to note that, despite the influx of corn—which from a classical market-based economic theory, should result in lower prices of corn produced products such as tortillas—tortilla prices have increased dramatically since the inception of NAFTA.[43] In response to hardships caused by structural adjustment, the Mexican government initiated food assistance programs, such as Progresa, to alleviate the costs incurred by poor consumers. Under the 1997 Progresa program, the Mexican government provides a 110 peso stipend instead of tortillas to female heads of household. In theory, this stipend should allow Mexican households to mitigate increased food prices for certain goods (in this case tortillas), providing them with supplementary income that can be used to purchase substitute foods, whether out of choice or out of taste preference. However,

poor consumers in Mexico who participate in Progresa may in fact purchase cheap US food products rather than the staple tortilla. But to portray this as a choice or a reflection of "consumers' taste" is to subscribe to the myth of social and cultural commensurability nascent in the market metaphor, a myth that is encouraged by the money being offered as food to the Mexican campesinos. It is to ignore the social, economic, and cultural contexts in which these particular Mexicans exist.[44]

Today, a new crisis is emerging in the tortilla industry as demand for maize is experiencing another spike as a result of hording and speculation by agro-industrial monopolies, rising costs of fuel, and international demand for corn for ethanol use.[45]

As described above, one of the requirements of IMF and World Bank structural adjustment was the privatization of national industries. With respect to grain, prior to NAFTA, Mexico's National Company of Popular Subsistence (CONASUPO) had been a relatively functional state monopoly. However, with the inception of NAFTA in 1994, the Mexican government decentralized CONASUPO and allowed foreign competitors to take control of the grain industry. As major market corporations such as the Mexican-based Maseca and the U.S.-based Cargill vied for control of the corn market, emphasis shifted from national sustainability to competition. This had particularly disastrous effects on local mill and factory owners as production increasingly moved into the hands of large producers.

One result of the concentration of production and distribution processes is the increased potential for corporations to manipulate supply and demand for profit-making purposes. Speculative practices are made possible under free-market environments in which corporations have the power to withhold or flood the market with, in the case of Mexico, corn. By speculating on domestic and international crop prices these corporations can manipulate market prices without regard for the people affected by price fluctuations. For the Mexican people, the types of policies instituted through structural adjustment programs, coupled with the corporate takeover of the grain industry, have had a dramatic effect on tortilla prices. Since the inception of NAFTA the price of tortillas has increased dramatically, per capita consumption has declined, and overall quality of life has deteriorated. This had led many to conclude that "today we are experiencing a new tortilla war, which . . . is being fought by the large agro-industrial corporations against the poor."[46]

While the World Bank has released reports that are critical of certain SAPs, it is still unclear whether the Bank's internal criticisms have translated into substantive policy or strategy reform. Critics of the Bank point to a larger problem inherent to the Bank itself. Namely, the structure of such a massive international lending agency is susceptible to both internal and external corruption. While it would be an exaggeration to claim that corruption is rampant in the Bank, reports have suggested that "corrupt practices of one type or another may be associated with more than 20 percent of the funds disbursed by the bank each year," an amount upwards of U.S. $4 billion.[47] Problems with corruption fall on both sides of the lender/debtor relationship, whether in the form of Bank economists or bankers receiving kickbacks, payoffs, or bribes, engaging in collusive bidding and embezzlement, or recipient governments engaging in corrupt practices.[48] In the 1990s the Bank initiated a series of internal investigations in an effort to curb internal as well as debtor country corruption. While these sweeping changes exposed some corrupt projects and attempted to make project loans more transparent, the Bank remained vulnerable to corruption. For example, most of its audit reports and internal operations reports still are rarely made public.[49] Couple this with the fact that the Bank's top 24 executive directors are legally bound to antidisclosure policies of what goes on in Bank proceedings, it is increasingly difficult to monitor internal corruption.

Another problem with fighting corruption involves the sheer number of claims the Bank receives. Despite efforts to address these claims, there is still a backlog of hundreds of cases. Key corruption cases include Kenya's Urban Transportation Infrastructure Project, Guinea-Bissau's Urban Transportation Infrastructure Project, India's Reproductive and Child Health Project, Lesotho's Highlands Water Project, Bolivia's Rural Investment Project, and various projects in Indonesia and Bangladesh. The Bank is a massive loan institution that is not necessarily bound by the same legal constraints as other governmentally regulated organizations. Moreover, the lack of transparency makes it hard for the general public to clearly see how funds are dispersed, which projects are allotted funding, and how these projects are selected for funding. Ultimately this leads to the issue of the Bank's effectiveness in dealing with one of its original missions: eliminating hunger. The Bank's failure to live up to its goals is important for a number of reasons. First, failed projects due to corruption or poor allocation of funds are counterproductive to the cause. Second, funds that do not make it to projects hurt both investors and the poor who they are designed to help. Finally, we must ask how the anti-democratic structure of the Bank lends itself to a logic of personal advancement. If officials increasingly face the possibility of personal advancement either through bribery or special interest lobbying, then massive amounts of funds may be lost.

Ultimately, the Bank suffers from two major problems, one on a conceptual level and one on practical policy level. On a conceptual level, critics such as Joseph Stiglitz argue that the Bank needs a fundamental change in governance. Of particular importance are voting rights. Both the Bank and the IMF need to implement voting rights that are more representative of and attuned to the needs of developing countries. Instead of listening only to the voices of the trade and finance ministers of the most powerful economic nations, the Bank needs to restructure its governance framework so as incorporate the perspectives of developing nations.[50] Along similar lines, although the Bank does recognize failures in its past policies, it needs to be more rigorous in evaluating those failures and facilitating ways in which developing nations can better participate in creating policy.[51] Regardless of whether the Bank acknowledges policy failures, it must continue to look at historical precedents that served to create the problems it is facing today. Restructuring policies based on the same economic concepts of free market competition, efficiency, and growth may only perpetuate these problems. While these issues are addressed more in the next chapter, the theoretical contrast the food sovereignty movement presents is worth mentioning here. Critics of current multilateral institutions have pointed to alternatives to a purely economic vision of globalization and the policies that are derived thereby. Rather than focusing simply on economic solutions to global poverty and food security (and attending theoretical concepts of competition, efficiency, and global trade), an alternative paradigm focuses on concepts of cooperation, environmental and self-sustainability, and local trade. However, before returning to these alternative themes, the following section investigates how the IMF also represents a purely economic understanding of globalization.

IMF AND THE FINANCIAL ARM OF DEVELOPMENT

Recalling the discussion in the first chapter, the IMF currently recognizes its three main objectives as surveillance, technical assistance, and financial assistance. Despite the IMF's original intentions to establish global-financial stability, Joseph Stiglitz identifies a change in its original mission. At its inception, the IMF operated under the economic theory that markets did not always function properly and that a global managing body was needed to provide economic stability.[52] Along these lines, the IMF believed that international pressure needed to be foisted upon countries to encourage expansionary economic policies. Today the Fund has changed courses and now generally provides funds to countries that implement contractionary economic policies. The ethos of the Fund today is one of optimism rather than skepticism, namely that free markets do in fact work successfully, and the most effective policies are those that promote the free market.

Central pillars of privatization, liberalization, and macroeconomic stability are all strategies that, similar to the World Bank, have come under fire for their shortcomings. As we have seen, the idea behind privatization is that in some industries, competing private enterprises can perform services in an efficient manner. In the 1980s and 1990s, unfortunately, the IMF (and World Bank) pursued rapid privatization policies with the above mentioned optimism, yet with the myopic view that markets "will emerge quickly to meet every need" of social adversity.[53] With respect to liberalization, and specifically trade liberalization, the general belief was that a country's economy would be enhanced "by forcing resources to move from less productive uses to more productive uses."[54] That is, comparative advantage would generate the most efficient labor and production schemes. We have already seen the failures of trade liberalization strategies of the World Bank. Again, the problem lies in the fact that the transition to more efficient markets does not always follow a fluid or seamless path. Liberalization practices are all the more damaging when developing countries are forced to open their markets while industrialized countries such as the United States and Europe continue to protect certain markets and industries. Finally, the IMF operates on the assumption that macroeconomic stability and growth can be achieved with the aid of foreign investment. The belief is that when corporations enter developing countries (or any country for that matter) they contribute to the local economy. Again, this is not always the case. Similar to the outcome of flooding food markets (e.g. dumping of food produced lower than the cost of production), when corporations enter local economies they often drive out local business. Opening developing and least developed markets to foreign corporations has had particularly damaging effects on local economies with respect to food and agriculture. The following case study examines the Monsanto Company as an example of both the increasing power of transnational corporations and their harmful effects on local agricultural practices.

CASE STUDY: MONSANTO AND TRANSNATIONAL FOOD CORPORATIONS

According to estimates in 1986, upwards of 85–90 percent of global agricultural trade was controlled by five companies.[55] The Monsanto Corporation is one of the major players in agricultural biotechnology, genetic seed production and patenting, and chemical (herbicide and pesticide) products.

Monsanto has strong ties with the U.S. government. For example, Supreme Court justice Clarence Thomas was Monsanto's lawyer prior to the first Bush administration. A former U.S. secretary of agriculture was on the board of directors of Monsanto's Calgene Corporation. Former Secretary of Defense, Donald Rumsfeld was on the board of directors of Monsanto's Searle pharmaceuticals. Two congressmen, Larry Combest, former Chairman of the House Agricultural Committee, and John Ashcroft were the recipients of Monsanto's largest political donations in the 2000 election.[56]

Along with its corporate and political clout, Monsanto has an annual budget of U.S. $10 million and a staff of 75 people solely devoted to investigating and prosecuting farmers that the company claims have infringed upon its patent rights.[57] Monsanto's rise to corporate dominance has occurred through three main business strategies. First, it has bought or merged with most of the major seed companies in an effort to gain control over seed germplasm. Second, it has numerous patents on genetic engineering techniques and genetically engineered seed varieties, thus dominating the market in biotechnology crops. Finally, it has required that farmers who purchase Monsanto seeds first sign an agreement prohibiting the saving of seeds (a practice that farmers around the world have done for centuries), thereby forcing them to buy Monsanto's seed every year.

Monsanto's most successful technology is its Round Up Ready plants. These plants are engineered to be tolerant to the Round Up herbicide. Farmers can spray their crops with Round Up, which fends off natural predators (e.g. butterflies, moths, caterpillars, etc.), without harming the crop. There are currently four major crops for which Monsanto has developed its Round Up Ready technology: soy, cotton, canola, and corn. Monsanto's market dominance in the United States is evidenced by the fact that as of 2004, "this technology accounted for 85% of all soy acreage, 45% of all corn acreage, and 76% of cotton acreage."[58] This is making it increasingly harder for farmers to find conventional varieties of seeds of these crops.[59] Saving seed allows farmers to prevent soil erosion and cultivate a greater gene pool from which other farmers and breeders can select seeds.[60]

Not only has Monsanto received criticism for its genetic research, it is also criticized for a ruthless war it has waged against those who challenge its patents and gene technology. For example, the infamous *Monsanto v. Schmeiser* case has drawn international attention. Percy Schmeiser, a family farmer in Canada, was accused of illegally cultivating Monsanto's Round Up Ready canola seeds. In 1997, Schmeiser vowed that he found a strand of canola plants in a ditch on his farm. Upon discovering this growth, Schmeiser sprayed the crop with an herbicide, only to discover that the crop was resistant to his treatment. Schmeiser later found out that five neighboring farms had purchased Monsanto's seeds. Monsanto first received word of the Schmeiser contamination from a toll-free snitch line the company had set up to encourage reporting of seed theft. After receiving this information, Monsanto conducted what it called an audit, which in reality was the hiring of a private investigator to extract samples from Schmeiser's land. However, documents from court proceedings revealed that Monsanto ordered investigators to *trespass* on Schmeiser's land to obtain these samples.

From the onset of the allegations, Schmeiser contended that the Monsanto seeds had blown over from neighboring farms or had fallen off delivery trucks en route to these farms, a claim that was warranted by the fact that Schmeiser's field tests revealed lower contamination levels deeper into his crop fields. However, lower Canadian courts rejected Schmeiser's claim that the canola landed on his fields by accident. Ultimately, Canada's highest court ruled in favor of Monsanto, saying that while the company cannot patent higher forms of life (i.e. the plant) it does retain patent rights over the gene.[61] In the end, although the courts ruled that Schmeiser did not have to pay Monsanto profits earned from the 1998 crop, the decision marked a decisive victory for the biotechnology industry. While Schmeiser's case was considered a minor victory insofar as he did not have to pay Monsanto's legal fees, other farmers have not fared as well. Monsanto rarely discloses its lawsuit and settlement figures, but estimates show that from 1997 to 2005 Monsanto won more than U.S. $15 million in judgments.[62]

Farmers around the world are protesting against Monsanto and large biotechnology firms and agribusinesses on the grounds that patenting genetically modified seeds infringes on time-honored agricultural practices. Farmers have always saved seeds both in an effort to cultivate the most genetically valuable (i.e. natural genetic selection) seeds, and as a security measure for future crop harvests. Moreover, farmers have always traded and exchanged seeds with each other. Companies such as Monsanto suggest that food security and hunger reduction will be achieved through food biotechnology rather than traditional farming practices. Alternatively, local, small-scale farmers argue that biotechnology in the hands of TNCs and their attendant patenting practices have not provided the world with more food. Instead, they have introduced harmful chemical pesticides and fertilizers that not only require expensive, capital intensive farm inputs, but are also environmentally destructive. Moreover, as we have seen, the concentration of agricultural sectors promotes monocropping and mass production, which destroys rural and sustainable farmer livelihoods.

Monsanto and other agribusinesses, at best, represent another example of a food security logic that disenfranchises global farmers in favor of corporate production, profit, and monopolization. At worst, Monsanto's massive market monopoly, its political clout in the United States and beyond, and its desire to control, manipulate, and patent seeds, represents the archetype of a global food system gone awry.

Ultimately, one of the most poignant conceptual problems with the IMF boils down to its belief that "what the financial community views as good for the global economy is good for the global economy and should be done."[63] This is all the more distressing given that

a key operating principle of the IMF and the World Bank is that of 'development' through private corporate investment in Third World countries. Yet the fundamental aim of corporations is to make profits for their shareholders, not to foster development or democracy in the poor areas of the world. A private investor (individual or corporate) makes investments in another country for one central reason: in order to take out more than was put in.[64]

This is part and parcel of the IMF losing its original vision. By succumbing to a corporate logic that fundamentally operates under the profit motive, and asserting that global financial management is the only means to macroeconomic stability, the Fund serves to complete a multilateral triad (i.e. WTO, World Bank, IMF) that promotes a purely economic understanding of global integration. With respect to the guiding question of this chapter, the IMF represents another multilateral organization that views the purpose of growth and development in economic terms. While the end goal of financial growth may involve the alleviation of poverty, the Fund's current policies, like the policies of the WTO and World Bank, prove otherwise. Its support of privatization, trade liberalization, and deregulation, albeit with a financial focus, make it complicit with the harmful policies instituted by these institutions. As the financial arm of global economic governance, the IMF serves to coordinate the monetary aspect of the triad and, as such, solidifies the purely economic understanding of global integration in which food security attempts to achieve its goals.

SUMMARY

The investigation in this chapter has highlighted some of the problems associated with the current conception of food security defined within the broader theories and policies of the UN, WTO, World Bank, and IMF. In response to the theoretical and policy failures of these agencies, local farmers and food rights activists have begun to voice their grievances. Both the concept of global governance institutions and the policies they promote have been exposed for their failures to improve food security on the one hand, and how they prove economically, culturally, and agriculturally harmful to the world's farmers on the other.

As Philip McMichael suggests, "Long discounted by the industrial fixation of developmental theorists and planners, food (and its security) looms as a force that threatens the current hegemony of the market. In fact, one might venture to suggest that food is as much a force to be reckoned with as money."[65] The surge in food riots in the last two decades testifies to the fact that current forms of globalization and the theory and practicality of a purely economic free market is contested ground. Critics have situated the question of global food relations in terms of "the crisis of development." On the one hand, over the course of the 20th century, development has become synonymous with industrialization, derived in part by the Industrial Revolution and culminating in national-industrial rivalries such as between the United States and the Soviet Union, and currently between the United States and the European Union. In the context of national-industrial rivalries, food was "removed from its direct link to local ecology and culture" and became important only to the extent that it generated industrial progress, mainly through its contribution to urban diets. On the other hand, the concept of development itself has garnered critique insofar as multinational organizations (as well as powerful industrialized countries) regard developmental growth as the panacea of social and economic problems. As multilateral organizations exercise increased influence on global economic integration, the strategies of development and growth have been displaced from their historical location in the nation-state (i.e. development as a national project) to the global arena.[66] With respect to food and agriculture, this displacement is evidenced through policy platforms such as those developed in the Uruguay and Doha rounds of the WTO, in which agriculture, food, and trade have come under the auspices of global governance.

Alongside the influence of multilateral organizations, the role of transnational organizations also deserves critical scrutiny. The emergence of monopolistic agricultural corporations is due in large part to the structural adjustment and free trade policies of the World Bank and WTO. Agribusinesses have been influential lobbyists for the implementation of global rules of trade and have advocated for the reduction of tariffs, the "harmonization of food standards," and stronger international protection of corporate intellectual property rights.[67] The influence of TNCs as a unit of analysis is a decisive theme in the current global politics of food, and point of contention with respect to how influential global corporations are with respect to food security. As Heffernan and Constance point out, the unit of analysis for the global food regime has changed, and depends on the topic being researched. In a discussion of labor issues and the impact on rural communities, a specific commodity (and its relations to the labor process, etc.) should be examined. If the theme pertains to regulatory issues of the agriculture and food system, the unit of analysis should be the nation-state. Finally, if the focal question concerns the driving force behind restructuring of the global food system, the unit of analysis has to be transnational corporations.[68]

In a similar vein, McMichael contends that the contemporary "food regime" and the current global development project instituted primarily through the WTO's Doha round cannot be divorced from the emerging role of powerful global corporations.[69] The strategic negotiations of Northern governments and the evolution of market-based economic solutions to global food networks by the WTO further demonstrate the emerging role of TNCs. For example, leading up to the Cancun Ministerial (2003), Northern states ventured on a more aggressive platform for implementing Doha reforms, whereby the Doha round was seen "as an opportunity to impose a corporate agenda of equal domestic treatment of foreign corporations, notably in private investment in public services, in return for Northern action in ending subsidies."[70] However, recalling the WTO's Green Box (non-trade distorting subsidies), the reformulated Cancun platform allowed Northern states to continue to dump cheap farm produce on to the world market. Ultimately, the Doha round served to amplify "international tensions and the contradictory relations which constitute development" because the round envisioned "global deregulation as the premise of development."[71] As outlined in chapter one, this vision was the culmination of the post-WWII, U.S. model of global food production and distribution whereby food aid was sent to Third World countries in an effort to simultaneously reduce U.S. food surpluses and alleviate food shortages in Third World and Southern countries. As Northern colonies began to break up over the course of the 19th century, the new vision of development sought to incorporate "post-colonial states into a universal system of national accounting methods, standardizing the measurement of material well-being (GNP)" whereby "only monetized transactions were counted as productive." This paradigm "devalued subsistence [farming], cooperative labor, indigenous culture, seed saving," and management of "the commons." As workers increasingly migrated to urban areas, this geographical displacement also resulted in "the displacement of customary forms of knowledge and moral economy."[72]

In the next chapter, the critiques of the food security model as conceived by the WTO, World Bank, and IMF, as well as current models of neoliberal and developmental growth, are juxtaposed with the emerging concept and movement of food sovereignty. As both a concept and a movement, food sovereignty represents an alternative to the way we conceive of almost every issue discussed within the topic of food security.

CHAPTER 3

Food Sovereignty as an Alternative

INTRODUCTION

The previous two chapters offered an examination of current neoliberal and developmental conceptions of food security, focusing specifically on how the concept is understood or reinforced by multilateral organizations such as the UN, World Bank, WTO, and IMF. These chapters also demonstrated that the manner in which we conceive of food security influences our larger perspectives on economic and cultural globalization and poverty. In response to decades of policy failures, the concept and accompanying movement of food sovereignty has emerged as a powerful counter voice to current visions of agricultural reform, farming, and globalization. This chapter begins by defining the concept of food sovereignty. Following this discussion, it details some of the central components of the concept, including small-scale agriculture, farmer to farmer knowledge sharing, agroecology, and the role of seeds and looks at themes such as competition versus cooperation and mutual versus foreign food dependency.

La Via Campesina, or the International Peasant Movement, founded the concept of food sovereignty. The organization is composed of "peasants, small- and medium-sized producers, landless [peoples], rural women, indigenous people, rural youth and agricultural workers" from around the world, including 56 countries in Europe, Asia, and the Americas. It was established as a world organization in May of 1993 in Mons, Belgium and up to date has held conferences in Tlaxcala, Mexico (1996), Bangalore, India (2000), and Sao Paolo, Brazil (2004) and Maputo, Mozambique (2008). Its founding purpose is to "develop solidarity and unity among small farmer organizations in order to promote gender parity and social justice in fair economic relations" through the implementation of agricultural practices that preserve "land, water, seeds and other natural resources," and foster sustainable agricultural practices based on small and medium-sized producers.[1] Furthermore, food sovereignty endorses sustainable agriculture based on family or peasant-based farm models that utilize local resources "in harmony with local culture and traditions." Finally, food sovereignty seeks to produce goods for "family consumption and domestic markets." While the original definition of food sovereignty has evolved since the movement's official inception, the core elements have remained the same. Currently, *La Via Campesina* offers the following definition of food sovereignty:

Food sovereignty is the RIGHT of peoples, countries, and state unions to define their agricultural and food policy without the "dumping" of agricultural commodities into foreign countries. Food sovereignty organizes food production and consumption according to the needs of local communities, giving priority to production for local consumption. Food sovereignty includes the right to protect and regulate the national agricultural and livestock production and to shield the domestic market from the dumping of agricultural surpluses and low-price imports from other countries. Landless people, peasants, and small farmers must get access to land, water, and seed as well as productive resources and adequate public services. Food sovereignty and sustainability are a higher priority than trade policies.[2]

Food sovereignty advances and augments many of the criticisms brought against neoliberal and developmental economics, agricultural reform, and food security.

Based on the analysis in the last chapter, we can now juxtapose current conceptions of food security and a purely economic understanding of globalization with a more culturally and politically attuned understanding of globalization, global hunger, and poverty. While the previous chapters identified the problems with a purely market-based notion of globalization, we have yet to clearly explain what a more *culturally sensitive* or *politically energized* notion of globalization would look like. Instead of attempting to establish a universal definition of culture, this chapter looks at how food sovereignty identifies with certain cultural practices and political struggles that challenge current trends in globalization. This method has several advantages. First, investigating the livelihoods of landless, subsistence, and small-scale farmers illuminates a particular contrast to the livelihoods of people in industrialized, wealthy countries. Agrarian people and their communities are not categorically different than the people and communities in industrialized, First World countries; rather, they embody cultural traditions, practices, and so forth that are increasingly marginalized by current trends in economic globalization. In fact, many of the same cultural practices (and the values, traditions, etc. associated with these practices)—

such as subsistence farming, sustainable development, local production for local sale, environmental protection, and so forth—are endorsed, yet marginalized, in industrialized countries as well. Although context differs, the marginalization process in industrialized countries can also be attributed to many of the same trends in corporate monopolization of agriculture, and in the policies of the World Bank, WTO, and IMF.[3] Second, by examining the food sovereignty movement, broader cultural values that can be contrasted to the cultural values implicitly and explicitly expressed in current models of economic globalization and food security emerge. Finally, a critical examination of food sovereignty reveals the complex and heterogeneous makeup of peasant, family, and small-scale agricultural communities. Understanding the heterogeneity, complexity, and subjectivity of these communities alongside the diversity of the cultural values, traditions, and customs they embrace allows us to avoid romanticizing these cultures as a sort of bygone cultural remnant of simple, pure living. Moreover, it helps us avoid conceiving of these communities as passive subjects of the globalization process. By investigating the political, cultural, and social values of food sovereignty we accomplish two objectives. On the one hand, we see that current models of globalization are not embraced by a large portion of the world. On the other hand, we see food sovereignty as an active and empowering movement that is meaningfully, and in some instances successfully, challenging the current direction of economic and cultural globalization.

To begin examining these issues, some preliminary distinctions can be made between food sovereignty and a food security model based on neoliberal and developmental visions of globalization. Food sovereignty's primary emphasis on local production for local consumption is underscored by a notion of interdependence. A focus on local, community development in which the interests of families, friends, and neighbors is extremely different than a neoliberal vision of a globally integrated world composed of rational, autonomous, self-interested individuals. Along these lines, purely economic concepts of competition, efficiency, profit-making, and unfettered consumption can be contrasted to concepts of cooperation, efficient production for local communities, mutual well-being, and sustainable development. A critical reflection on these complex themes can begin with some of the specific ideas and practices advanced by food sovereignty activists. The following section examines the theme of small-scale versus large-scale global agriculture.

SMALL-SCALE LOCAL AGRICULTURE VERSUS LARGE-SCALE GLOBAL AGRICULTURE

Critics of market-led agricultural reform identify numerous problems with World Bank and WTO-sponsored policies for the agricultural sector. They point out how trade liberalization, privatization, deregulation, import/export models, and free trade policies have resulted in the spe-cialization and homogenization of local agricultural sectors. Attendant to these policies is the consolidation of small-scale, family, and self-sufficient farms into large-scale farms that practice monocropping, employ capital intensive methods of production, produce for export, and harm biodiver-sity. While market-led, neoliberal models suggest that large-scale agricul-ture is apt for providing food security, food sovereignty advocates argue that large-scale farming will neither feed populations properly nor gener-ate widespread rural prosperity.

The idea that small, family farms are "backward, unproductive and inef-ficient," and ultimately an obstacle to economic development, has been challenged by many food sovereignty activists.[4] Instead, food sovereignty activists argue that mounting evidence reveals that small farms have mul-tiple functions that benefit both society and the biosphere. Challenging the premise that market-led reforms produce more efficient farms, small-scale producers are fighting against the idea that they should be incorpo-rated into large-scale farms and export production schemes. According to market-led reform theories, small-scale and peasant farmers may experi-ence some unfortunate side effects of industrializing agriculture. The task, therefore, for multilateral organizations, NGOs, and other civil society or-ganizations is to make this transition as seamless and painless as possible. Part of the belief that small-scale farms are inefficient is based upon a sub-tle yet significant understanding of efficiency.

Peter Rosset shows how an economic model that measures *total output* versus *yield* generates different results with respect to efficiency. A neo-liberal model that measures yield by gauging "the production per unit area of a single crop" fails to address how monocropping leaves empty land space (niche space) that small-scale farmers utilize for other crops. Third World farmers are more likely to engage in intercropping methods in which empty spaces are utilized for planting other crops. In large-scale, mecha-nized models, empty spaces are required for machines to harvest large tracts of land, whereas on small-scale, individually tended farms, these spaces can be utilized. As such, measuring efficiency in terms of yield of a single crop may prove higher for large-scale farms, but if the measurement is in terms of total output; namely, the output of all crops on a designated plot—including various grains, fruits, vegetables, fodder, animal products, and so on—small-scale farming is more efficient.[5] If measured in these terms, small farms actually make more efficient use of land than large-scale farms.

While it is important to note that small-scale farms make efficient use of land, the discussion on efficiency can potentially divert attention away from the ways in which farming contributes to other aspects of farmers' livelihoods. Although small-scale farming does have economic impor-tance for farmers, the question remains how a purely economic conception of productivity and efficiency serves to reduce farm products to abstract, economic commodities. By focusing on how farming serves other purposes such as "the overall improvement of rural life—including better housing, education, health services, transportation, local business diversification, and more recreational and cultural opportunities," we begin to see the cultural importance of agrarian life.[6] Food sovereignty activists recognize the total benefits of small-scale agriculture by focusing not only on economic gains, but also on how small-scale agriculture promotes biodiversity, connects farmers and families to the land, and provides an intimate link between farmers and the crops and foods they produce and consume.

AGROECOLOGY

Agroecology is both a developmental concept and practice that centers on small-scale, family, and peasant farming. While farmers have engaged in agroecological methods for millennia, the concept and practice of agroecology has gained renewed interest in response to failed policies of the Green Revolution and neoliberal agricultural reform. Agroecology is based on local, traditional agricultural knowledge, environmentally safe and culturally significant sustainable development, organic rather than capital and chemical intensive inputs, and biodiversity. As a science, agroecology strives for a deep understanding of ecosystems, such as how plant and animal life interact with the human production of foods and resources. In other words,

agroecology is the holistic study of agroecosystems, including all environmental and human elements. It focuses on the form, dynamics and functions of their interrelationships and the processes in which they are involved . . . Implicit in agroecological research is the idea that by understanding these ecological relationships and processes, agroecosystems can be manipulated to improve production and produce more sustainably, with fewer negative environmental or social impacts and few external inputs.[7]

Agroecology is an important practice given that a large portion of the world's poor (370 million) live in areas that are resource poor and located in remote regions or risk-prone natural environments. To compensate for these obstacles, agroecology builds upon local knowledge of land and farming. Through different farming techniques—depending on regional differences in geography, climate, water availability, and so on—farmers can creatively utilize their natural surroundings to increase biodiversity, generate year-round crop yields, and avoid harmful and costly chemical inputs. Moreover, agroecological techniques help to regenerate the land, which allows for conservation for future generations.

Agroecology seeks to utilize the natural environment as a means to optimize farming capabilities and output. Agroecological technologies generally employ the following processes: (1) recycling biomass and balancing nutrient flow and availability; (2) securing favorable soil conditions for plant growth through enhanced organic matter and soil biotic activity; (3) minimizing losses of solar radiation, air, water, and nutrients by way of microclimate management, water harvesting, and soil cover; (4) enhancing species and genetic diversification of the agroecosystem in time and space, and; (5) enhancing beneficial biological interactions and synergisms among agrobiodiversity components resulting in the promotion of key ecological processes and services.[8]

The technical aspects of agroecological sciences are outside the scope of this project, but what is important to note is the manner in which agroecology differs from neoliberal and developmental perspectives of agriculture. Rather than focusing simply on high-yield agricultural methods, which often rely on monocropping techniques, agroecology utilizes the resources available to local farmers. Not only has research revealed that agroecological methods are more productive than high-input systems in terms of output per unit area, it has shown that they are more biologically diverse and environmentally conservationist. Moreover, agroecology provides farmers and families with the labor and sustenance suitable to culturally important livelihoods.[9] In many ways food sovereignty embodies the tenets of agroecology insofar as it emphasizes the small-scale, local potential of agriculture. Agroecology utilizes regionally appropriate natural resources such as land, water, vegetation, and animal life, which allow farmers to develop their local agricultural potential. The food sovereignty call to organize "food production and consumption according to the needs of local communities" by giving priority to production for local consumption resonates well with agroecology.

SEEDS

Alongside small-scale farming and agroecology, food sovereignty has rallied behind issues involving seeds. Seeds are the building blocks of agriculture and have been shared, naturally adapted, and stored for future use by farmers for millennia. As Vandana Shiva notes, "Seeds are a gift of nature, past generations, and diverse cultures," the "first link in the food chain, and the repository of life's future evolution."[10] While not directly linked to the macroeconomic policies of multilaterals, the issue of seeds is particularly important for food sovereignty because the seed industry represents one of the fastest growing areas in which corporate monopolization is destroying the lives of millions of farmers. Given that the top three seed companies (Monsanto, Dupont, and Syngenta) account for 47 percent of the worldwide proprietary seed market and the top 10 seed companies account for 67 percent of the global proprietary seed market, the corporate takeover of the seed industry is one of the largest contributors to the loss of seed biodiversity.[11] The FAO estimates that crop genetic resources are currently decreasing at a rate of 1–2 percent annually, which is due in large part to the acceleration of intensive agriculture and the replacement of genetic diversity by fewer high-yield crops, all trends facilitated by current neoliberal and developmental policies for food security. For example, while India once cultivated upwards of 30,000 different varieties of rice, now only 30–50 varieties exist. In China, the cultivation of 10,000 different wheat varieties has been reduced to 1,000, and in the Philippines, where over 6,000 varieties of rice were once nurtured, Green Revolution varieties "occupy 98 percent of the entire rice-growing area."[12]

The exchange or barter of seed is also a vital activity of peasant and small-scale farmers. In an effort to resist certain trends of globalization, including corporate monopolization, the patenting of seeds, and agricultural reform that usurps land and territory, food sovereignty struggles to safeguard farmers' seeds. Food sovereignty and seed go hand in hand in the struggle for land and territory rights, and the capacity of agricultural workers to "produce, preserve and provide food" for its own people should constitute a sovereign right of the people. By destroying local agricultural production through corporate or governmental policies, local communities are increasingly forced to purchase imported grains, processed foods, and junk food—all unhealthy alternatives to traditional, locally grown foods. As an aspect of food sovereignty, the right to healthy, nutritious, and locally grown food is grounded in values of self-determination, dignity, freedom, justice, and equality. To put it another way, "In a neoliberal capitalist structure, a people that [sic] does not produce its own food (or a great part of it), is a people that can be easily subjugated by pressure, extortion or domination imposed by the trans-national empire and will end up losing its sovereignty."[13]

The current system is destroying biodiversity, including natural seeds, flowers, plants, animals, fish, waters, rivers, seas, minerals, and lands, as well as cultural diversity, including traditional knowledge, rituals, songs, poetry, traditions, eating habits, dress, dance, occupations, and crafts. For example, "Food enhances our capacity to create, and awakens our senses by its colour, taste and smell. It is also at the heart of our festivities and ceremonies, it encourages dialogue and sometimes [serves as] an offering of thanksgiving at funerals."[14] The corporate takeover of the seed industry not only intensifies the loss of biodiversity, but on a symbolic level marks a general lack of care for cultural diversity. As a symbolic aspect of food sovereignty, seed diversity represents the diversity of the world's farmers, farmers who cultivate different crops according to tradition, communal identity, and taste preferences.

The issue of seeds is also critical for female agricultural workers and activists as they represent a doubly marginalized voice in international food relations. Traditionally, these women have not only faced marginalization in their own communities through patriarchal family structures or communal status, but now they face the added hardships caused by neoliberal globalization. In many agrarian communities, women have the sole responsibility for raising children, caring for the home, and preparing meals alongside daily routines of helping out on the farm. It is estimated that rural women are "responsible for half of the world's food production, and they remain the primary producers of the world's staple crops (rice, wheat, and maize), which provide upwards of 90 percent of rural poor's food intake.[15] Regardless of the availability of income and food, women are responsible for the family's food security. With respect to seed, it is often up to women to select, collect, preserve, and plant seed, and, as such, any loss of seed diversity has disastrous ramifications for their ability to carry out family and farm responsibilities. To this extent, seed represents another element of the historical heritage and traditions of agricultural communities. As female food sovereignty activists argue, seed represents the foundation of food sovereignty insofar as it is inseparable from other basic necessities such as food, housing, and clothing.

The case study on the Zapatista movement in southern Mexico, while not initially affiliated with the food sovereignty movement, represents another example of social activism engaged with agricultural issues. On a broad level, the Zapatista movement fights for the same sorts of economic, political, and cultural rights as the food sovereignty movement. On a specific level, the movement represents a forum for women to voice their struggles for equality, justice, and solidarity. Both the Zapatista and food sovereignty movements represent an emerging plight of women's rights. While both of these movements are still a long way from realizing the full extent of gender equality, they demonstrate how the challenge of current neoliberal models of globalization by food sovereignty is opening up new forums for voicing historical injustices and marginalization.

CASE STUDY: THE ZAPATISTA UPRISING

The Zapatista uprising in southern Mexico on January 1, 1994 captured the global attention of a broad spectrum of people, including similar indigenous social movements, the mass media, agriculture movements, and Northern governments. While the roots of the social and political marginalization that spawned the uprising date back 500 years to the Spanish conquest of Mexico, the 1994 uprising was founded upon many of the themes voiced by the food sovereignty movement.[16]

The uprising came on the heels of the United States/Mexico-sponsored implementation of NAFTA in 1994. While the specific date for initiating the conflict was less a symbolic demonstration against the trade agreement and more a strategic move that required tactical maneuvering and strategy adaptation once the first struggles caught the attention of the Mexican government, the symbolism gained potency once the uprising garnered support from other social justice movements around the world. Originally, the uprising was a response to years of marginalization by colonial powers, neoliberal economic policies, and oppression by the Mexican government. Armed with a litany of real and symbolic weapons, from sticks, hand-carved wooden guns, machetes, and small ammunition, the Zapatistas took control of many towns in the Chiapas province in southern Mexico. The Zapatistas donned black ski masks and colorful bandanas that represented various historical Mexican heroes, such as Emiliano Zapata and Pancho Villa, and that have become internationally recognized as symbolic attire. The enigmatic and charismatic spokesperson for the struggle, Subcomandante Marcos, announced the initial inspiration of the uprising:

Hoy Decimos Basta! Today we say enough is enough! To the people of Mexico: Mexican brothers and sisters: We are a product of 500 years of struggle, first against slavery, then during the War of Independence against Spain led by insurgents, then to promulgate our constitution and expel the French empire from our soil, and later [when] the dictatorship of Porfirio Díaz denied us the just application of the Reform laws . . . We have been denied the most elemental education so that others can use us as cannon fodder and pillage the wealth of our country. They don't care that we have nothing, absolutely nothing, not even a roof over our heads, no land, no work, no health care, no food, and no education. Nor are we able to freely and democratically elect our political representatives, nor is there independence from foreigners, nor is there peace, nor justice for ourselves and our children.[17]

While this statement was released immediately following the initial uprising, the Zapatistas's demand for land, housing, education, and health care have remained the central issues around which they rally. Currently, the Zapatistas have released six Declarations of the Selva Lacandona (the region where they are located), all of which address these basic humanitarian needs. Not only do Zapatista press releases, or communiqués, outline their grievances, they also call upon other indigenous and social justice groups to join in solidarity for similar causes.

As the Sixth Declaration of the Zapatista National Liberation Army (EZLN) notes:

What we want in the world is to tell all of those who are resisting and fighting in their own ways and in their own countries, that you are not alone, that we, the zapatistas, even though we are very small, are supporting you, and we are going to look at how to help you in your struggles and to speak to you in order to learn, because what we have, in fact, learned is to learn . . . And we want to tell the Latin American peoples that we are proud to be a part of you . . . And we want to tell the people of Cuba, who have now been on their path of resistance for many years, that you are not alone, and we do not agree with the blockade they are imposing, and we are going to see how to send you something, even if it is maize, for your resistance. And we want to tell the North American people that we know that the bad governments which you have and which spread harm throughout the world is one thing—and those North Americans who struggle in their country, and who are in solidarity with the struggles of other countries, are a very different thing. And we want to tell the Mapuche brothers and sisters in Chile that we are watching and learning from your struggles. And to the Venezuelans, we see how well you are defending your sovereignty, your nation's right to decide where it is going. And to the indigenous brothers and sisters of Ecuador and Bolivia, we say you are giving a good lesson in history to all of Latin America, because now you are indeed putting a halt to neoliberal globalization.[18]

The Sixth Declaration outlines many of the economic and political struggles the Zapatistas wage against neoliberal economic development. It is a unifying message, not intent on violent revolt, but rather on vigilant resistance to harmful governmental and multinational economic policies, corrupt domestic and transnational corporate practices, and the imposition of foreign cultural norms and values.

Along these lines, and similar to the food sovereignty movement's call for egalitarian agricultural reform, the Zapatistas represent the plight of many peasant and subsistence farmers in southern Mexico. The vast amount of land in this region is used for agricultural purposes, with the cultivation of maize and coffee representing the two principle crops. With respect to coffee production, the structural adjustment programs of the early 1980s had especially harmful effects on the Chiapas region, when coffee prices declined as a result of the Mexican government failing to implement support mechanisms (production quotas) for coffee producers.[19] The majority of producers in this region are small-scale producers (two hectacres or less), and on average during the 1989–1993 period overall production fell by 35 percent and small producers suffered a 70 percent drop in income as a result of poor macroeconomic management by the Mexican government. This resulted in thousands of small producers abandoning production.[20]

Similar experiences occurred in the maize industry. Macroeconomic reform cut subsidies to the agricultural sector, and with Green Revolution-sponsored modernization policies, farmers faced increased input costs as well as declining access to credit. As a result, the percentage of farmers operating at a loss increased to 65 percent by 1988. While some small-scale producers were able to weather these changing economic conditions—because they were able to rent farm land to agricultural workers and receive some credit packages from the Mexican government—subsistence farmers were unable to maintain production. Deteriorating economic conditions also proved environmentally destructive as farmers were forced to accelerate the clearing of delicate rainforests to produce for survival. Again, these macroeconomic policies were a direct result of World Bank-sponsored structural adjustment reforms that conditioned loans on radical agricultural sector reform, including the reduction of price supports and other input subsidies, which would have lessened the harmful impact on small-scale and subsistence producers.[21] The culmination of agricultural reform with the implementation of NAFTA served to subordinate these farmers to the imperatives of free trade.

Under these conditions the Zapatistas garnered support from local, indigenous, and peasant farmers calling for the Mexican government to recognize the plight of the rural poor, indigenous peoples and agricultural workers. In essence, the Zapatistas represented a local democratic movement fighting against the imposition of harmful trade agreements, multilateral policies of deregulation and privatization, and the opening of the agricultural sector to free trade. In response to the Zapatista uprising and their attendant grievances, the Mexican government organized the San Andrés Accords in 1996 to discuss indigenous and cultural rights. Initially the Mexican government vowed to recognize the collective rights and autonomy of indigenous groups and agreed to forge new constitutional rights whereby indigenous groups were, on the one hand, represented in the national government, and on the other, allowed to govern their own regions.[22] Despite the progressive promises of San Andrés Accords, the Mexican government ultimately rejected these reforms, causing the Zapatistas to take matters into their own hands.

By 2003, after losing hope that the Accords would come to fruition, the Zapatistas endeavored to create their own autonomous municipalities in which regional governance would be directed by the people in the jurisdictions. The EZLN refers to these autonomous municipalities as the "Juntas of Good Governance"—as opposed to "bad" governance (i.e. The Mexican government). These juntas serve to mediate issues between municipalities, as well as encourage agroecological projects of sustainable agricultural development.

Aside from political demands, activists from the Zapatista movement and *La Via Campesina* reiterated their solidarity in fighting for women's rights, justice, and equality. Zapatista women reaffirmed their right to participate in revolutionary and community decision making regardless of their "race, creed, skin color or political participation." They demanded the right to work and receive fair compensation for their labor. They demanded the right to hold political office if elected freely and democratically. Furthermore, they reaffirmed their right to be afforded basic necessities such as access to primary medical care, education, and to be treated as dignified beings in which they live free of physical and mental abuse.[23]

While many of these basic demands seem obvious and second nature, they have not been afforded to millions of marginalized and oppressed women. As increasingly visible forums for voicing social justice demands, the Zapatista and food sovereignty movements represent a strategic and potentially powerful means for women to articulate their grievances. Not only do these women connect concepts of food sovereignty to the survival of their families and communities, they also negotiate local gender rights issues within their specific communities. The right to food and the struggle for global recognition of this right will not be accomplished without the support and activism of rural, peasant, and indigenous women.

COOPERATION VERSUS COMPETITION

One of the complex themes in both neoliberal and developmental models of food security specifically, and globalization in general, is cooperation. As we have seen with UN organizations such as IFAD and the FAO, there is mounting rhetoric on the need to coordinate policy strategies with field researchers and local communities. From a developmental perspective, IFAD, for example, acknowledges the need to cooperate with local communities in crafting policy that will improve the management of natural resources, utilize new technologies, and improve the ability of agricultural producers to compete in competitive agricultural markets. However, evidence shows that policy coordination ultimately needs the input of IFAD field workers to either determine what sorts of programs are needed or to impart knowledge of current trends in the global economy. Moreover, how new technologies will function efficiently and productively, as well as how natural resources should be appropriated for sustainable development, are coordinated by field workers.

As a process of cooperation, policy coordination that includes the input of both IFAD and the communities it works with, for example, ultimately boils down to integrating these communities into larger macro level or international markets. This is demonstrated, for example, in the practice of microfinancing, whereby field projects attempt to create economic infrastructures that allow people to engage in economic relationships based on competition, efficiency, and profit-making to afford the rural poor the potential to secure a better standard of living. However, as the last chapter illuminated, microfinancing is problematic on several levels, the most important being the fact that it works only in certain contexts and for specific purposes.[24] Ultimately, what is critical for food sovereignty activists is the way these types of models and programs promote a form of cooperation that is utterly foreign to many of food sovereignty's agricultural communities.

The same challenges are posed to the multilateral organizations of the WTO, World Bank, and IMF, albeit on a more critical level. While developmental models promoted by the UN are ostensibly making an attempt to incorporate community participation, food sovereignty argues that, historically, multilateral organizations have implemented policies based patently toward macro level and international economic growth and development. For these multilateral institutions, competition, efficiency, and profit-making are incentives that should include not only local community members but national businesses and TNCs. To this extent, economic growth and development should not be delimited to how economic policies improve poverty conditions, but should also include how the market in general prospers. Namely, while curbing poverty may be one objective, it is only one objective among many that serve to generate wealth, bolster industry, and modernize rural communities. Basing policies on these theoretical foundations begs the question of how competition potentially pits community members against each other and splinters relations. Similarly, as we saw in the last chapter, the notion of efficiency must be weighed against the downsides of monocropping and the destruction of biodiversity. And, finally, profit-making diverts attention away from sustainability and toward unfettered production and consumption. A critical reflection on themes of efficiency, competition, and profit-making must address alternative ways of understanding these concepts, namely, ways in which they can be used that are not destructive to community relationships. Food sovereignty both implicitly and explicitly demonstrates how these concepts function differently in certain agrarian settings.

For example, while cooperation is often important for family and community survival, it also illustrates a profound understanding of human interdependence. As illustrated in the concept of agroecology, for example, cooperation is not only a way to share successful agricultural techniques, but is also intertwined with community gatherings, sharing food, and establishing solidarity through new friendships. The notion of competition is a little more difficult to analyze. It would be egregious to suggest that all small-scale, peasant, and family farmers dismiss competition in favor of a form of cooperation that leaves families and communities with low income, a low standard of living, and no chance to improve their socioeconomic conditions.

However, a differentiation between a corporate logic of profit maximization and a more benign sort of competition deserves further exploration. For example, food sovereignty activists challenge the industrialization of agriculture propagated increasingly by an agribusiness logic that focuses intently on the consolidation of land, jobs, and wealth. As was addressed in the previous chapter, the growing strength of agribusinesses such as Monsanto is creating a new corporate landscape in which the logic of mutual, community cooperation is replaced by a corporate logic that operates according to its own internal standards and principles. As Jerry Mander notes, "The corporation . . . operates by a system of laws and inherent structural rules that leave it utterly beyond the norms of human 'morals,' of concerns for community or for the harms that may be caused by industrial activity . . . The corporation operates by an internal logic containing certain guidelines: economic growth, profit, absence of ethics and morals, and the endless need to convert the natural world into industrial processes and commercial products."[25] Despite the fact that some corporations include ethical standards for business operations, this endless need to industrialize illustrates how a corporate logic guided by profit and the conversion of the natural world into commercial products is in many ways diametrically opposed to a community-based logic of mutual interdependence and cooperation. Critics of a corporate logic of competition are correct in identifying how corporations operate according to standards that may not apply to other forms of human relations.

To take the example of food production and consumption, the corporation can be contrasted to the family unit. From an agribusiness agenda, food production involves implementing the most efficient, high-yielding, and profitable means to introduce a product into the market. Whether the consumer decides to purchase the product is simply a matter of economic supply and demand. Although corporations strive to supply desirable food products, consumption is ultimately divorced from the production process. Whether due to import/export models that deliver goods from thousands of miles away from consumers, or corporate strategies that provide only a certain variety of foods, consumers are increasingly oblivious to the purchasing choices they make, as well as to how these choices impact farmers. Alternatively, we could look at the production-consumption cycle of food in the household. Setting aside for the moment the example of subsistence farming, whereby the entire production-consumption cycle is contained within the family unit, let us look at a traditional household meal.[26] Even though purchased foods may be shipped long distances, once the ingredients enter a household and are ready for preparation, a new, micro-level production-consumption process begins. Families share production duties such as setting the table, preparing meats and vegetables, and so forth. Furthermore, this time may serve as a communal gathering during which family members bond with each other, tell stories, laugh, and reminisce. To a certain extent this is a process of culture formation as these gatherings function to shape and reshape how we identify as siblings, parents, in-laws, community members, and so on. Obviously this is a somewhat simplistic example, but the stark contrast between this type of production-consumption cycle and that of the corporate model is worth noting. If we extend this example to include the peasant- or family-based farm, the production-consumption cycle is all the more intimate. Not only is food prepared and consumed together, but the entire family participates in the physical planting, cultivation, and harvesting of the food needed for meals. Given that 70 percent of the world still lives in such agricultural settings, this comparison is all the more germane.

A reflection on the difference between cooperation and competition provides insight to how food sovereignty advances a radically different perspective on cooperation. Ultimately, cooperation should neither be conceived as between governments, multilateral organizations, and TNCs, nor between UN field workers and local communities, but rather, between local family and community members. For example, the *Campesino a Campesino* movement's ethos is illustrative of how food sovereignty conceives of mutual, community-level cooperation. From an outside perspective, many of its methods may seem unorthodox given different ideas of efficiency, knowledge sharing, and cooperative labor; however, the *Campesino a Campesino* movement demonstrates alternatives to the idea of cooperation envisioned by the multilateral organizations we have examined thus far. An analysis of the movement provides one example of how grassroots organizers coordinate agricultural projects with minimal aid from outside organizations.

EL MOVIMIENTO CAMPESINO A CAMPESINO: MUTUAL VERSUS FOREIGN FOOD DEPENDENCY

El Moviemiento Campesino a Campesino (the Farmer to Farmer Movement or MCAC) embodies nearly every theme promoted by food sovereignty. The movement emerged out of land reform movements in Central America in the 1960s and represents a model of agrarian life that challenges macro-level modes of production and consumption on virtually every level.

In chapter one, we discussed how developmental organizations such as the FAO and IFAD have moved away from World Bank-sponsored types of agricultural development and economic knowledge transfer, a managerial form of knowledge transfer in which trained professionals simply dictate policies with respect to the implementation of new technology, agricultural reform, and economic development. Alternatively, the FAO and IFAD advocate for a more participatory process in which local farmers and community members also collaborate with field workers. However, as we elucidated in the last chapter, these participatory models still involve the expertise and recommendations of agency field workers. Given that projects must be approved by the FAO and IFAD project directors, the participation of local communities is adumbrated by a hierarchical organizational structure that determines what types of projects are pursued and how funds should be allocated.

Alternatively, the *Campesino a Campesino* movement embodies a categorically different form of knowledge sharing. In what Eric Holt-Giménez refers to as the *campesino* pedagogy, agricultural practices are shared with other farmers in a way that is reflective of a "deeper, culturally embedded exchange in which *knowledge is generated and shared* (my emphasis)."[27] *Campesinos* in Latin America (and increasingly in other parts of the world) are engaging in agroecological practices that incorporate the production of food and the protection of the environment.

The sharing of cultural wisdom produced a set of general normative principles that suggest that MCAC's technologies and methods are deeply rooted in meaning. Codified as a simple stick figure, MCAC is said to 'work' with two hands: one for production of food and the other for protection of the environment. The Movement 'walks' on the two legs of innovation and solidarity. In its 'heart' it believes in love of nature, family, and community, and it 'sees' with a vision of campesino-led, sustainable agri-cultural development.[28]

This symbol of the *campesino* farmer represents a model for farming that challenges many of the strategies imposed by Green Revolution-sponsored agriculture and development. Beginning in the 1960s and 1970s in Latin America, the Green Revolution implemented agricultural techniques that were capital-intensive, had high external inputs, and that utilized fertile agricultural land for single crop production (monocropping).[29] These techniques required extensive training, expert management, and the use of heavy machinery, pesticides, herbicides, and fertilizers. While Green Revolution experts acknowledged that these practices would alter rural agricultural sectors, ultimately, efficient production and increased yields would provide the world with greater food security. Although some peasant and small-scale farmers would be forced off their land into wage labor (often in urban environments), in the long run this would be an inevitable process of globalization and industrialization.

The MCAC, alternatively, promotes a farmer- or people-centered approach to agriculture, which, on the one hand, challenges centralized, hierarchical models of agricultural research and policy implementation, and, on the other hand, allows these farmer networks to generate their own local knowledge of agriculture and development. For example, through the use of farmer-organized workshops, *encuentros* (gatherings), and *intercambios* (exchanges), farmers from local and regional areas participate in agricultural experimentation and share knowledge of successful agricultural techniques. Workshops are generally organized around hands-on activities in which farmers gather in the field to share and experiment with methods of efficient, sustainable, and productive farming. Describing these workshops illuminates the cultural elements of these gatherings:

Classroom sessions are punctuated by songs, stories, jokes, poems, sayings and games. Sometimes a local band is invited to play music during the break periods. Food is simple but *must* be abundant. Alcohol is usually prohibited during the taller [workshop], but often the last evening ends in a big party, sometimes lubricated with the local brew. Frequently, farmers putting on or traveling to the workshop come from far away, sometimes from other countries. Strong friendships are established that over time weave dense networks of reciprocity and solidarity.[30]

During *encuentros*, which are more formal in nature, peasant and small-scale farmers gather to share their individual experiences and debate the most successful strategies for sustainable development. In the less organized *intercambios*, voluntary groups of farmers gather to generate interest in experimental agricultural techniques as well as get to know other local farmers.[31] Through these workshops, gatherings, and exchanges culture is formed and reshaped in a mutual cultural praxis in which "agriculture technologies are adopted and adapted, spread and modified, not through extension of exogenous information and techniques, but as part of a process of endogenous agricultural expression."[32]

The *Campesino a Campesino* movement serves as yet another example of how food sovereignty challenges current neoliberal notions of top-down agricultural management, foreign dependency, cooperation, and a purely economic notion of human relations. Moreover, the successes of the movement demonstrate a viable alternative to World Bank, IMF, and WTO policies that are utterly foreign to these cultural values and practices. To contrast some of these themes, the World Bank's 2008 report on agriculture and development proves illuminating.

The report's analysis of genetically modified foods and the role of agribusiness demonstrates two important areas in which food is conceived as a purely economic commodity, and sustainable development is appropriated by a neoliberal understanding of globalization. With regard to genetically modified foods, the Bank suggests that genetically modified crops hold great potential for pro-poor development. Although the risks and benefits of these technologies need to be assessed, and countries should have the freedom to decide whether they want to deploy these technologies, the Bank emphasizes how these technologies have benefited many developing countries. The rhetoric employed in the report pays lip service to counter arguments on the use of genetically modified foods, but ultimately highlights the potential for these technologies to feed the world's poor. Simply offering countries the 'choice' whether or not to utilize these technologies avoids questions regarding the circumstances in which countries and their rural farmers are making these decisions. If these people are not informed about the potential pitfalls and dangers of genetically modified foods, such as how health risks are still under dispute, how genetically modified foods require more capital and chemical intensive inputs, and how genetically modified seeds reduce biodiversity, they may not fully understand the implications of utilizing these technologies.

The Bank's vision for agribusiness follows a similar line of reasoning. Current trends in the concentration of agribusiness power and market control have revolutionized the way agribusinesses influence the food supply chain; production, distribution, and marketing; and the availability of culturally important foods. Although the Bank acknowledges the need to incorporate small-scale producers as well as enforce corporate responsibility, its final emphasis is on how to integrate small-scale producers into larger markets. This focus underestimates the influence of enormous transnational agribusinesses. The emerging corporate consolidation of seed, chemical fertilizers, and pesticides is rapidly undermining the ability of small-scale farmers to compete both in their local markets and in larger state and international markets.[33] In sum, the consolidation of corporate control in agriculture and chemical industries, which goes largely uncontested by the Bank, undermines the capacity of family and peasant farmers to, one the one hand, choose which crops they want to cultivate and, on the other hand, maintain control over their local agricultural industries. These trends in genetically modified crops and agribusiness represent two areas in which the Bank continues to undermine the plight of rural and small-scale farmers. Moreover, agribusiness practices are completely alien from the methods of the *Campesino a Campesino* movement. To bring these themes into focus, the case study "Biofuels: The New Manipulation," illustrates how corporate monopolization and marketing is attempting to re-inscribe themes of sustainable development and environmental protection into the corporate logic of capitalism. Following this case study is another one on the MST movement in Brazil. This movement is particularly important insofar as it embodies many of the same themes promoted by food sovereignty activists and serves as an example of a social movement that is taking radical measures to promote their demands.

CASE STUDY: BIOFUELS: THE NEW MANIPULATION

As an emerging response to global environmental, climate, and natural resource crises, as well as a specific U.S. and corporate strategy to oblige a growing demand for more environmentally healthy and sustainable energy use,
the biofuels industry and its attending movement have garnered increasing
criticism from farmer and food rights activists around the world.

Biofuel technology and production is based on the idea that exploring new
ways to harness energy from our natural resources can be a more "clean,
green, and sustainable assurance about technology and progress."[34] By moving attention and dependency away from oil-based and other finite resource
energy production, the biofuel industry argues that it is developing inno-
vative alternatives to current energy consumption. Proponents of biofuels
claim that harvesting renewable fuels such as corn, sugarcane, soy, and other
crops will provide alternative energy sources that will reduce environmental degradation and dependency on nonrenewable energy resources. Biofuel
advocates argue that these energy sources are environmentally clean and
green, will not result in deforestation, will promote rural development, and
will not increase global hunger.

In reality, however, activists are drawing attention to the harmful side effects of the move toward biofuels. Despite the fact that cultivating fuel crops
can reduce greenhouse gasses in the atmosphere and reduce fossil fuel consumption, when we take into consideration the entire process—from land
clearing to consumption—the record shows that greenhouse emissions from
"deforestation, burning, peat drainage, cultivation and soil-carbon losses"
counter original gains.[35] Contrary to claims that biofuels will improve rural
development, with the invasion of large agribusinesses seeking to take advantage of this market, small-scale rural farmers are increasingly pushed off
their lands, similar to those processes we examined in the first two chapters.
Finally, the claim that the production of biofuels will not impact world hunger is discredited by the fact that the world's poor generally spend between
50 to 80 percent of household income on food. As the demand for biofuel
crops intensifies competition for land and increases world food prices, the
poor will suffer the brunt of these changes. Citing statistics from the International Food and Policy Research Institute, Eric Holt-Giménez notes that
estimates suggest world food prices in staple goods will increase 20 to 33 percent by 2010, and 26 to 135 percent by 2020, which will dramatically cut
down daily caloric consumption of the world's poor.[36]

Ultimately, the demand for biofuels hides the social, economic, and political implications of these new technologies and practices. Food activists
point to how the biofuel boom will disproportionately benefit U.S. and European consumption patterns. For example, in 2007 the U.S. congress signed
the Energy Independence and Security Act, which sets a *"mandatory Renewable Fuel Standard (RFS) requiring fuel producers to use at least 36 billion gallons
of biofuel in 2022."*[37] This represents a five-fold increase in current levels
of biofuel usage. This mandate will invariably have ecological and socio-
cultural implications for developing countries as the United States ventures

into agricultural markets to achieve these goals. Imports of palm oil from Southeast Asia and Latin America, as well as sugarcane ethanol and biodiesel from Brazil, will continue to increase market-based land reforms, the transition to monocropping, and the influence of powerful corporations, all of which amplify and perpetuate many of the food security problems discussed in the first two chapters.[38] While the RFS is subject to change, as it stands now, U.S. support for biofuels will continue to harm the communities directly involved in biofuel production.

Alongside disproportionate consumption levels by industrialized nations, the biofuel industry is also increasingly coming under corporate consolidation, leading many activists to coin it the "agro-fuels" industry. Currently, large corporations control about 60 percent of production in agro-fuels (primarily corn-based ethanol). However, studies on the future trends in agro-fuels production estimate that market control will be increasingly held by a few major corporate players. For example, in June of 2007, Monsanto announced a 70 percent increase in third quarter profits, due largely to an increased demand for corn seeds used in ethanol production.[39] Given that "90% of U.S. ethanol comes from corn and most of the U.S. corn crop is genetically modified, ethanol has earned itself the nickname of "Monsanto moonshine"—Monsanto Corporation being the leader in GM [genetically modified] corn as well as other genetically modified crops."[40]

As an issue of food sovereignty, reducing land traditionally used to cultivate corn, soy, sugarcane, and other staple crops, or allocating disproportional crop yields for other purposes such as biofuel production will in turn reduce supply to local communities and raise prices. As outlined in the previous chapter, by restructuring local agricultural systems to produce for export or other macroeconomic demands, biofuel production will reduce land currently dedicated to producing food, and thus make the world's poor more vulnerable. Increasing food scarcity in basic food staples and making domestic economies more subservient to TNCs and global economic market trends undermines food sovereignty. Instead food rights activists argue that "the right to food, the basic fuel of living beings, is of a higher order than the need to fuel machines."[41]

CASE STUDY: MST: TAKING MATTERS INTO THEIR OWN HANDS

Brazil's Landless Workers Movement (MST) is composed of 1.5 million landless workers who struggle for social justice, genuine land reform, and peasant and small-farmer rights. Beginning in 1985, the MST has peacefully reoccupied and cultivated unused Brazilian land for the purpose of peasant, small-scale, and family farming. Land ownership in Brazil is particularly unbalanced, with three percent of the population owning almost two-thirds of the total arable land. Since MST started re-occupying unused land, it has won land titles for over 350,000 families and currently 180,000 encamped families await government recognition.[42]

While the MST has gained the recognition of the Brazilian government, its successes have not been without cost. Organizers and landless people regularly confront the police, military groups, hired gunman, and the courts, often incurring violent beatings, imprisonment, and death. However, rarely do members break the law; rather, they attempt to uphold government promises to redistribute land in a more equitable fashion. According to the Brazilian Constitution, in order for land to be legally obtained, it has to serve its social function. Although the government has made promises to make this social function conceptually relevant, powerful local landowners (and their foreign allies) have thwarted reoccupation efforts through intimidation, legal manipulation, and violence. Taking matters into their own hands, the MST began to occupy lands in the 1970s by establishing encampments. Establishing encampments usually begins with MST organizers identifying a large group of landless peoples who could potentially establish an encampment on a piece of land that is held under terms that can be legally contested. Upon first settling, people are usually forced off the land by hired gunmen or locally corrupt police working for the land tenant. Life on burgeoning encampments is usually very difficult, as settlers face constant threats alongside day to day conditions of extreme poverty, hunger, and disease. These hardships are amplified by the fact that, for successful reoccupation, the MST must resolutely remain on these lands until the Brazilian government or courts decide to grant ownership. This process usually takes between two and four years, during which the settlers face the above mentioned dangers. While life on the encampments is difficult, through the support of other MST cooperatives, church groups, labor unions, and sympathetic political leaders, these encampments have proved increasingly successful, and have demonstrated to the world the vision of the MST.

Currently, the MST has created "sectors" or "collectives" that organize projects and promote policy pertaining to specific issues, including "production, cooperation, education, environment, gender, political education, health, culture, communications, human rights, [and] youth."[43] With respect to production, cooperation, and environment, the MST has created agricultural production cooperatives, both collective and semi-collective, in which local farmers produce on common lands for the benefit of the entire community. On an infrastructure level, the MST has created its own credit operations (banks) that serve the local borrowers and producers and help manage financial procedures. It has established small- and medium-scale food processors for the processing of fruits, vegetables, dairy products, cereals, meats, and sugar. It has launched an Environmental Education Campaign to beautify settlements by planting trees, flowers, forests, and gardens. And, it has trained local farmers in agroecology, including environmentally safe methods of production, as well as the cultivation of natural, organic seeds.

With respect to political education, the MST has created regional and state schools to teach settlers about the conditions the rural poor face in Brazil. These educational centers, whether in local schools or at small communal gatherings, train individuals in awareness about the realities of landless farmers and workers, how to sustain long-term MST presence in the countryside, and how to craft more egalitarian agricultural reform policies. For example, in 1997 the MST created the Technical Institute for Education and Research on Agrarian Reform (ITERRA), which offers courses in technical administration of cooperatives, social communication, and community nursing and health care, among others. Educational opportunities on the encampments continue to grow, and currently the MST has 40 partnerships with 13 universities.[44]

Similar to women's rights struggles characteristic of the food sovereignty movement and the Zapatista movement, part of the MST effort to create a more just and equitable society involves the participation of women. The organization has a "gender sector" that strives to end gender inequalities through the establishment of "new economic, social, political and environmental relationships" that are "based on values such as respect, friendship, solidarity, justice and love."[45] Initiatives include the guarantee of child-care services at all MST gatherings so as to ensure women are not excluded due to child care responsibilities. The MST is also dedicated to equal representation of men and women in all educational and training activities, and it attempts to guarantee one male and one female director in each community. The MST also attempts to document the lives of rural working women, thus contributing to grass roots record keeping of the lives and efforts of community members. Finally, as an integral aspect of education, the MST is dedicated to incorporating the theme of gender relations and equality in their entire curriculum. While MST members admit that gender parity is still a work in progress, the fact that its founding mission inscribes the rights of women illustrates how food sovereignty and its similar reform movements are struggling to create more just and equitable gender relations.[46]

In an effort to improve the health care of MST communities, the organization also fights for access to quality medical care, and attempts to grow and utilize herbal medical treatments for MST communities and encampments. Since the MST's inception, the health care "sector" has trained community health care educators, implemented a HIV/AIDS prevention program, and helped record the quality of life and housing conditions of thousands of families.

Similar to the Zapatista utilization of the mass media, the MST has also established outlets for communicating their cause. The MST's regular publication, the Sem Terra Journal, was released over two decades ago and remains one of the longest published journals for a popular resistance movement in print. The MST also works with local university radio stations and controls many medium range transmitters used to broadcast events. The Sem Terra Journal is representative of the Sem Terra people (landless), and speaks for the impoverished, the unemployed, those without rights, and those who suffer cultural, political, and economic marginalization.

As one of the most active and influential social justice groups in the world today, the MST embodies yet another example of the global challenge to neoliberal economic theory, and World Bank, WTO, and IMF-sponsored development models of economic globalization. The MST is representative of similar global movements that seek inclusion in the legal, economic, and political life of national governments. In Brazil, the MST has garnered wide-spread public support from sympathizers, and has captured the attention of the Brazilian government.[47] By struggling for a more just society in Brazil specifically, the MST has also brought attention to many of the same struggles advocated by food sovereignty. The movement embodies a peaceful assertion of human rights generally, and farmer, landless worker, and peasant rights specifically. By confronting current neoliberal economic and corporate visions of globalization, the MST has not only presented a symbolic challenge to these visions, but also a practical and substantive alternative to current conceptions of globalization, hunger, and poverty.

CONCLUSION: A NEW DIRECTION FOR FOOD SECURITY

The concept and movement of food sovereignty presents a challenging critique of the current neoliberal and developmental concept of food security. As a concept it proffers a particularly incisive criticism of the way food security is conditioned by the World Bank, IMF, and WTO, as well as the increasing corporate monopolization of the food and agriculture industry. As a movement, it clearly embodies alternative values such as cooperation, efficiency in terms of local productivity, and interdependence. By promoting practices such as local production for local consumption, agroecology, and sustainable development, the MST movement embodies an alternative to current economic concepts of globalization. While UN organizations such as the FAO and IFAD recognize the shortcomings of World Bank, IMF, and WTO policies, the current definition of food security still falls short of outlining the demands voiced by food sovereignty. The FAO is even beginning to question its current focus on poverty reduction as a means to eliminate hunger and malnutrition. It is beginning to question whether we must tackle the problem of hunger before we address the issue of poverty.[48] As such, the food sovereignty movement holds a critical and strategic position in terms of theorizing policy implementation for issues of hunger and malnutrition.

Although the definition of and policies for food sovereignty continue to evolve, we can summarize the most central issues in discussion. The International Planning Committee for Food Sovereignty (IPC) provides a synopsis of the issues discussed in this chapter. Food sovereignty includes the following elements: alongside the basic right to food, agricultural production should focus on local production for local consumption, and small-holder farmers and landless people should be afforded better access to land, water, seeds, and livestock. Moreover, farmers should be protected from patents on seeds, livestock breeds, and genes. Common resources such as water should be considered public goods that are distributed equitably, and sustainably used. With respect to agricultural reform, it must be genuine reform in which land distribution is equitable, and in which smallholder farmers are allowed to decide what they consume and how and by whom what they consume is produced. Part of this effort will involve the right of countries to protect themselves from under-priced agricultural and food imports, as well as the elimination of all forms of dumping. In other words, countries should be allowed to exercise the right to impose taxes on excessively cheap imports. Additionally, farmers, and specifically female farmers, need more avenues to participate in local agricultural policy decision-making. According to food sovereignty, these goals can be accomplished through agroecological methods that provide the potential for achieving sustainable livelihoods and environmental conservation.[49] These basic proposals outline the specific nature of the demand for food sovereignty, which here refers to how people choose to live, what and how they choose to produce and consume, and how to construct a more just, equitable, and democratic world.

Recalling the methodological proposal at the beginning to this chapter, these demands also highlight important implications for how we conceive of the current global food system. Policies of agroecology, small-scale farming directed toward local production for local consumption, cooperation, and sustainable development, challenge ideas of competition and efficiency in terms of mass production for export, profiteering, and unfettered growth. In the global North, people are starting to voice similar concerns. In the United States, for example, people are beginning to articulate concern over the fact that on average our food travels 1,300 miles from production to processing to our dinner plates.[50] This disconnect from the production process all but ensures a reduction in purchasing choices as the global corporatization of the food industry increasingly dictates what is available on supermarket shelves. Not only has the global North lost awareness of, for example, seasonal foods, but consumers are increasingly unaware of how their purchasing decisions detrimentally impact millions of farmers abroad.

The final objective of analyzing food sovereignty on its own terms is to better understand the heterogeneity, complexity, and subjectivity of these communities. Moreover, by understanding this movement on its own terms, we acknowledge that the movement should not be understood as a sort of bygone cultural era of simple, pure living. We recognize that the movement is not simply rejecting processes of globalization, but rather calling for legal, economic, and political rights that challenge the fundamental grounding of how we conceive of themes such as justice, equality, and democracy. This is palpably visible, for example, in food sovereignty's commitment to women's rights. As Raj Patel notes, "The commitment to women's rights, and the acknowledgement that the food system depends on women's work, from seed development to harvest to cooking to serving, is one of the clearest signals that some farmers' movements aren't pining for some rustic past, but want to shape a radically different future."[51] The last two chapters in this book address how food sovereignty represents a unique social movement in which community, political, and cultural rights are intertwined with the issue of food. This discussion ultimately leads to some broader ethical prescriptions for how we conceive of hunger and global poverty, and provides a lens through which we can potentially re-envision justice, equality, and democracy.

CHAPTER 4

Human Rights, Human Responsibilities, and the Capabilities Approach

HUMAN RIGHTS AS A FOUNDATIONAL DEMAND OF FOOD SOVEREIGNTY

Examining the continuum of neoliberal and developmental models of economic globalization on which conceptions of food security and food sovereignty fall serves as a fruitful ground from which to critique current forms of economic, political, and cultural globalization. While the food sovereignty model represents one aspect of theorizing how to better feed the world's agrarian and rural poor, it also introduces wider discussions on issues of global poverty and global social justice. Moreover, organizations such as the MST, the Zapatistas, *La Via Campesina*, and the Farmer to Farmer Movement, which advocate many of the ideals of food sovereignty, serve as remarkable case studies from which to examine the potential for social mobilization and social justice movements to challenge current trends of globalization.

Food sovereignty's foundational declaration that food is a human right involves the subsequent demand that peoples and national governments have a real and efficacious ability to define their agricultural and food policies. Given the focus in the first three chapters on the analysis of food security and food sovereignty on international, state, and local levels, the notion of human rights deserves investigation insofar as these rights represent a core demand of food sovereignty's struggle. Furthermore, human rights need critical scrutiny in terms of how they are conceived and function on state and international levels. This chapter introduces a discussion of the ethical implications of the food sovereignty and food security debate. It concentrates on how the challenges food sovereignty presents to neoliberal and developmental models of food security specifically, and globalization and poverty generally, raise ethical questions that shape the way we understand current models of globalization. Rather than attempting to develop a comprehensive ethic of social justice or an ethic of food, this chapter highlights several of the central ethical issues raised by food sovereignty in an effort to bring attention to how this movement contributes to broader themes of hunger and global poverty. In tackling questions pertaining to global poverty, one could also look at the role of inadequate health care, poor labor standards, and insufficient education to name just a few. While it is outside the scope of this project to address these issues, the ethical questions raised by food sovereignty apply to all of these problems. Focusing on the ethical issues presented by food sovereignty inevitably raises questions that apply to these broader issues of globalization and poverty, but a reflection on the specific questions raised by food sovereignty allows us to substantively address the topic of hunger and malnutrition, as well as clarify some of the challenges for policy implementation. This chapter focuses specifically on the topic of human rights with special attention to various ethical questions and problems associated with the language of rights generally and human rights language and implementation in particular.

Given food sovereignty's emphasis on food as a human right, this analysis sets the parameters for drawing connections between general human rights language and food sovereignty, which is examined in the final chapter. Following this discussion, the debate between cultural relativism and the universality of human rights is analyzed in an effort to address one major theoretical debate within human rights conversations. After this section the work of Thomas Pogge is analyzed as a proposal to suggest some more radical ethical implications of human rights in relation to global governance institutions such as the IMF, World Bank, and the WTO. Finally, the chapter concludes with a discussion of Amartya Sen's and Martha Nussbaum's capabilities approach and contends that this approach provides fruitful theoretical and policy content that can be applied to food sovereignty's cause.

THE LANGUAGE OF RIGHTS

The language of rights has a long tradition, and as Martha Nussbaum notes, there are diverse ways in which theorists approach issues about rights. People differ with respect to the basis of rights; namely, are rights conferred due to rationality, sentience, or mere life? Debate also considers whether rights are prepolitical, or present regardless of the juridical or political system an individual is in. Or are rights the construction of laws and socio-political institutions? Theorists also differ on whether rights apply to individuals, groups, or both. Furthermore, the language of rights also elicits debate on the relationship between rights and duties. Namely, if person or group A claims a right to X, is there a person or group B that has a duty to provide

X to person or group A?[1] To put it in terms of our present project, if food sovereignty claims a right to produce locally grown food, are governments, multilateral organizations, corporations, and so forth obligated to provide and secure this right? Given that the language of both food security and food sovereignty contains reference to the right to food, it is important to clarify how the language of rights will differ depending on whether the duty-provider is a government, multilateral organization, corporation, or all of the above.

Alongside these questions regarding the basis of rights, theorists have also made the distinction between positive and negative rights. Generally speaking, positive rights refer to rights that demand fulfillment, or require the *actions* of others (people, governments, etc.) to secure certain demands. Alternatively, negative rights describe our *freedom from* having something harmful or objectionable done to us.[2] Negative rights have also been couched in terms of noninterference. Conventionally, noninterference refers to the noninterference of governments; however, as is examined below, we can apply the concept of noninterference to entities such as multilateral organizations and transnational corporations as well. However, before looking specifically at the relationship between negative rights and the practices of multilateral organizations, we will evaluate one major ethical debate within discussions on human rights. Given food sovereignty's call for food to be considered a *human* right, it is important to ask if the movement demands a particular right or group of rights associated uniquely with their cause, or if their demands transcend the movement and apply to general concerns associated with globalization and global poverty. Specifically, the concept of human rights generates criticisms regarding claims to the universal nature of these types of rights. The modifier "human" in human rights indicates that these types of rights apply to all human beings regardless of "race, colour, sex, language, religion, political or other opinion, national or social origin, property, birth or other status."[3] These questions and issues bear directly on the debate between food security and food sovereignty insofar as both developmental agencies such as IFAD and the FAO and food sovereignty advocates argue that food is a human right.

CULTURAL AND ETHICAL RELATIVISM VERSUS THE UNIVERSALITY OF HUMAN RIGHTS

The debate between universalism and cultural/moral relativism plays an important role in theorizing human rights, rights that supposedly transcend national and international boundaries. A cultural relativism perspective holds that cultural values, traditions, beliefs, and so forth vary with respect to location and historical context.[4] Namely, if we look at different historical periods, the values, traditions, and beliefs differ, often drastically, from their counterparts in modern society. Moreover, if we examine modern cultures, we also find a diversity of values, traditions, and beliefs (that also had

different expressions within their historical periods). Given this phenomenon, cultural and moral relativists argue that it is impossible to determine
any *one*, universal set of values, traditions, or beliefs that transcend location and time. As such, any attempt to impose a universal system of values,
even in the most vague terms, such as those underpinning human rights—
the right to freedom, well-being, work, and so on—would constitute a dis-
respect of cultural difference. A violation, that is, if right's theorists are
committed to a high degree of reverence for cultural difference.

For instance, critics of human rights accuse human rights advocates of
imposing Western ideals such as freedom, liberty, and autonomy on other
cultures that do not necessarily hold these concepts as universally valuable.
A universal understanding of a human right presupposes consensus on certain cultural and social values, as well as how we should conceive of the
human qua human. Universal human rights, for example, as defined by the
UN, implicitly conceive of the human as a rational, autonomous, and self-
interested being whose main priorities concern the protection and promotion of freedom and liberty. This is implicitly evident, for instance, in the
UNDHR language, which states that human rights apply to every individual "regardless of discrimination of any kind as to race, colour, sex, language, religion, political or other opinion, national or social origin, property,
birth or other status."[5] While the rights language used in the UNDHR is
important in that it deems certain rights inviolable simply because we are
humans, it does not offer the context in which these rights apply to concrete
individuals or groups. Namely, if we assume a notion of rights that applies
regardless of race, sex, language, religion, and so forth, what does this
amount to? Does rights language become meaningless or empty if we attempt to impress its universal nature outside the scope of how different
people in different contexts obtain these rights?

To address these questions, the UNDHR suggests that human rights are
based on the equal dignity of all human beings. Alongside the UNDHR,
subsequent human rights documents such as the International Covenant
on Civil and Political Rights (ICCPR) and the International Covenant on
Economic, Social, and Cultural Rights (ICESCR) outline an extensive list of
human rights that are based on the dignity and worth inherent to all human
beings.[6] While the fundamental claim for human dignity is abstract in the
sense that it requires the addition of substantive policy, the ICCPR and the
ICESCR have made inroads into how cultural differences play a role in how
we conceive of human rights and how cultural diversity can potentially
contribute to the realization of human rights.

For example, the UN's Educational, Scientific, and Cultural Organization (UNESCO) has attempted to respond to some of the issues surrounding the implementation of human rights in different cultural contexts by
arguing that intercultural dialogue holds the best hope for a future of peace
and the longevity of diverse cultures.[7] UNESCO's Universal Declaration on
Cultural Diversity addresses the dilemmas posed by cultural relativism by

both outlining a definition of culture and by linking this definition to a more substantive promotion and protection of human rights. The document declares that "culture takes diverse forms over time and space" and that this diversity is "embodied in the uniqueness and plurality of the identities of the groups and societies making up humankind."[8] Cultural diversity and a general desire for a harmonious, peaceful world requires policies of inclusion and participation that respect this diversity.[9] A key challenge for realizing peace and harmony involves economic development, and, as such, UNESCO's Declaration argues that cultural diversity expands the range of policy options for "economic, intellectual, emotional, moral, and spiritual development."[10] Cultural diversity is also inseparable from human rights as outlined in the Vienna Declaration, Article 27 of the UNDHR, and Articles 13 and 15 of the ICESCR.[11] For example, the Vienna Declaration states:

All human rights are universal, indivisible and interdependent and interrelated. The international community must treat human rights globally in a fair and equal manner, on the same footing, and with the same emphasis. While the significance of national and regional particularities and various historical, cultural and religious backgrounds must be borne in mind, it is the duty of States, regardless of their political, economic and cultural systems, to promote and protect all human rights and fundamental freedoms.[12]

Article 27 of the UDHR states:

Everyone has the right to a standard of living adequate for the health and well-being of himself and of his family, including food, clothing, housing and medical care and necessary social services, and the right to security in the event of unemployment, sickness, disability, widowhood, old age or other lack of livelihood in circumstances beyond his control.[13]

Article 13 of the ICESCR highlights the educational facet of respect for cultural diversity, and notes that

education shall enable all persons to participate effectively in a free society, promote understanding, tolerance and friendship among all nations and all racial, ethnic or religious groups, and further the activities of the United Nations for the maintenance of peace.[14]

Education enables people to express themselves creatively, disseminate their artistic and creative productions, and participate fully in their specific cultural contexts. Article 15 notes the right of all people to "take part in cultural life," "enjoy the benefits of scientific progress and its applications," and "benefit from the protection of the moral and material interests resulting from any scientific, literary or artistic production of which he is the author."[15] These articles establish language both for rights pertaining to basic necessities and for rights pertaining to a more substantive expression of well-being. Moreover, successful developmental policy must draw from diverse cultural experiences and sources of knowledge.

While the incorporation of the ICESCR and the ICCPPR gives more substance to human rights as outlined in the UN's Universal Declaration of Human Rights, the question remains as to who has the duty or obligation to secure or provide these rights. Part of the problem is due to the fact that civil and political rights, despite the Vienna Declaration's insistence on their interconnectedness and interrelation, are still emphasized over economic, social, and cultural rights. The inclusive language in the ICESCR, which states that all signatories participate in the realization of these rights through mutual cooperation, indicates that the fulfillment of these rights is "not only for the benefit of persons within its jurisdiction but in the experience of individuals everywhere."[16] As such, each signatory country must recognize how its economic and social policies impact people outside the country. Accordingly, all signatory nations should "help construct a cooperative, mutually beneficial international economic order, one in which each member's policies and actions are influenced by consideration for the economic/social welfare of all peoples, not only those within its own national borders."[17]

This, however, is difficult to accomplish given that the rights outlined by the ICESCR are "open-ended" and are more difficult to codify than the rights outlined in the ICCPR. Historically, the

status and value of the Covenant [ICESCR] as a human rights guarantee was subjected to sustained critique on the basis that whereas civil and political rights were 'negative' rights requiring only abstention of the State from interference in designated spheres of an individual's life, socio-economic rights were 'positive' rights requiring the provision of goods/services to the individual by the State.[18]

As a consequence, civil and political rights are ostensibly easier to enforce through immediate legal channels, while economic, social, and cultural rights are subject to state discretion in terms of how these rights are conceived and implemented.

The current, dominant model of human rights, in other words, privileges negative rights, or the freedom *from* harmful or objectionable infringement on human freedom and liberty. States and international organizations are called upon to avoid impeding people's ability to exercise their freedoms and liberties, as well as to protect citizens against human rights violations. While civil and political rights are indeed important (as well as negative rights in general), Rajeev Patel argues that citizens under our current schema of human rights are reduced to "passive" participants. In other words, the public sphere is relegated to the status of watchdog as they participate in human rights issues. Their participation is limited to efforts of calling attention to violations after they have occurred. This model encourages activists to become outraged when human rights violations occur, to send letters to their governmental leaders, but ultimately confines activists and human rights organizations to "the role of orchestrator and conductor of the public's chorus of disapproval. It systematically cuts the general public out of the loop in terms of policy formulation."[19] In sum, the general public has forums to voice human rights violations, but does not have a robust platform from which to participate in the creation of human rights policy.

Aside from concerns about how current human rights language (and policy) pigeonholes activists into passive participation, negative rights theorists also highlight a problem Alan Girwith calls an "overload of duties."[20] Given, for example, the millions of people suffering from poverty, malnutrition, disease, homelessness, and so forth, a positive rights approach (or the duty to actively secure certain rights or objects of rights) invariably involves "unlimited, open-ended positive obligations that require drastic, indeed revolutionary, change in whole ways of life."[21] In other words, the inherent demands human rights place on individuals, governments, multilateral organizations, and so forth, make them palpably impossible to guarantee. This is a warranted concern that should not be underestimated. With respect to our current examination of food security and food sovereignty, given the fact that upwards of 840 million people suffer annually from hunger and malnutrition, how can individuals thousands of miles away and far removed from situations of extreme deprivation be held responsible for securing other people's right to food? To make matters more complex, is it feasible to not only provide food security, but to also realize food sovereignty's demand for healthy, culturally important, and locally produced foods? These questions are addressed in the final chapter, but deserve mention insofar as they highlight some basic problems associated with human rights.

While positive rights theorists understand these problems, their understanding does not weaken the moral dimension of their arguments. Regardless of the theoretical conundrums inherent to positive rights—not to mention the complexity of human rights policy implementation—the thrust and force of positive rights lie in the idea the we are morally obligated to help those in need. On a certain level, this moral obligation involves at least a consideration of positive duties. For example, Peter Singer's classic example of positive duties affords the principle that "if it is in our power to prevent something bad from happening, without thereby sacrificing anything of comparable moral importance, we ought, morally, to do it."[22] This argument is important conceptually, and applicable to more localized instances of protection of rights. Namely, in our local communities, we are better equipped to protect the rights of our neighbors, as well as possibly more inclined to forgo certain personal liberties or desires to aid immediate family, friends, or community members. However, Singer takes his argument one step further and argues that sacrifices of minor personal or community inconvenience also apply to international instances of poverty and aid.

According to Singer, given the increasing efficiency with which international aid agencies can disperse relief assistance, the proximity of individuals in need of aid does not diminish the force of this moral principle.

Unfortunately, Singer's contention here is somewhat optimistic and pragmatically tenuous. As we saw in the case study on food aid in chapter two, there remain enormous problems associated with the efficient distribution of international aid and the connection between famine prevention and political will power. As Alex de Waal demonstrates with respect to the specific issues of famine prevention and aid, we must also focus centrally on the role of political failures in poor countries if we want to understand the main causes of this aspect of global poverty. As opposed to corrupt and poorly managed international governments, democratic countries, or countries with basic civil and political liberties, such as democratic elections, free newspapers, and freedom of speech, are more likely to have institutions or mechanisms to prevent, and, if needed, alleviate famine. While de Waal does not confine all instances of famine prevention to the political realm, he does invite us to ask this question: How is a positive rights approach limited by our inability to influence the political regimes of countries experiencing extreme poverty? Instead of pointing one, definitive finger at multilateral organizations, or the inefficiency of aid work, we must also recognize how inept or corrupt political regimes fail or refuse to administer adequate famine prevention and relief services. While De Wall focuses specifically on the relationship between famine and poverty, his focus on failures in the political sphere draws attention to problematic aspects of a positive rights approach. If a positive rights approach calls for governmental intervention or the provision of certain basic necessities (much less the provision of cultural and economic rights), and foreign governments fail their own citizens, how are we, in more affluent countries, able to tackle both of these problems?

While the role of political willpower with respect to global hunger and poverty is somewhat outside the purview of our present analysis, what is important here is the way a positive rights approach introduces a moral claim on those who are better off. The application of positive rights holds fruitful theoretical considerations from which to ground moral claims on providing human rights, but in the end may prove too weak for implementing the massive and wide scale structural reforms needed to eliminate global hunger and curb poverty. With respect to the debate between food security and food sovereignty, the changing face of the global food relations requires a more in-depth analysis of how different actors—specifically the World Bank, WTO, and IMF—contribute to structural conditions limiting the realization of both food security and food sovereignty. Although these multilateral organizations are not the sole entities responsible for our current incapacity to substantively reduce global hunger and poverty, they deserve special attention due to their global reach. The following section offers a theoretical approach that meets many of the challenges to human rights discussed thus far.

GLOBAL GOVERNANCE AS A VIOLATION
OF HUMAN RIGHTS

As evident in the above discussion, UNESCO's Universal Declaration on Cultural Diversity, for example, contains language that suggests that a greater awareness of and respect for cultural diversity can complement how we understand human rights, as well as aid in the effort to find consensus within varied cultures as to what rights are considered *a priori* rights. Although UNESCO's Declaration is helpful insofar as it emphasizes state responsibilities to increase educational opportunities, promote equality, and provide basic necessities, its language remains within the confines of positive rights. As such, the document has minimal rhetorical force insofar as it does not provide specific solutions on how to guarantee these rights. To address this issue, Thomas Pogge offers a stronger notion of human rights by arguing that human rights should be considered in terms of negative rights. Given that it is difficult for everyday citizens to actively participate in the enforcement of human rights, we might begin, first, by giving human rights language stronger rhetorical force. In other words, if it can be shown that the current global economic and social order—whether due to the action or inaction of state governments, multilateral organizations, TNCs, or trade arrangements—perpetuates extreme poverty for hundreds of millions people, then we are indeed actively participating in massive human rights violations.

Pogge's account of extreme poverty and human rights suggests this is the case and, as such, provides a good first step in urging people to become active participants in the realization of human rights. By arguing that the current global economic order constitutes a violation of human rights, we are urged to critically reflect on how our choices, whether in the form of the political leaders we vote into power, how we understand the role of multilateral organizations such as the World Bank and IMF or trade arrangements promoted by the WTO, or the specific choices we make with respect to food consumption, actively contribute to a violation of human rights. The following section outlines Pogge's central argument with respect to extreme poverty and human rights. In the final chapter, we examine how the food sovereignty model, in turn, helps to provide some concrete applications for Pogge's theoretical account of human rights.

Pogge offers an intriguing analysis of global poverty and human rights by reorienting discussions on positive and negative rights and duties through a more radical conception of global justice. Taking a position that resonates with critics who dispute a purely economic understanding of human behavior, Pogge argues that the economic concept of *homo economicus*, or the idea that humans are rational and single-minded individuals who seek to optimize their personal preferences, is not a good description of reality.[23] In fact, this understanding of human nature functions, at best, only in economics departments, and, at worst, as the theoretical foundation of unjust global economic theory and practice. Therefore, Pogge focuses his discussion of global justice on the way current global governance institutions, such as the IMF, World Bank, and WTO represent global institutions that create and sustain human rights violations.

Pogge's approach begins with the basic fact of radical global inequality. For Pogge, radical inequality can be characterized by the following assumptions:

1. The worse-off are very badly off in absolute terms.
2. They are also very badly off in relative terms—very much worse off than many others.
3. The inequality is impervious: it is difficult or impossible for the worse-off substantially to improve their lot, and most of the better-off never experience life at the bottom for even a few months and have no vivid idea of what it is like to live in that way.
4. The inequality is pervasive: it concerns not merely some aspects of life, such as the climate or access to natural beauty or high culture, but most or all aspects of life.
5. The inequality is avoidable: the better-off can improve the circumstances of the worse-off without becoming badly off themselves[24]

If we agree that these conditions describe our current reality, then Pogge argues that severe poverty "manifests a violation by the affluent of their [the poor's] negative duties: an immense crime in which we affluent citizens of the rich countries (as well as the political 'elites' of most poor countries) are implicated."[25]

Pogge grounds his argument on the assertion that human rights specifically, and social justice in general, involves "solely negative duties" or "specific minimal constraints on what harms persons may inflict upon others."[26] He neither denies the existence of positive rights nor argues that positive duties are weak; rather, he contends that negative duties are more "stringent" than positive duties on the grounds that it is easier to defend the protection of negative rather than positive duties. Stated differently, with respect to poverty, Pogge's approach addresses criticisms of positive rights approaches that fail to distinguish between *causing* global poverty and *merely failing to reduce it*.[27] From a negative rights perspective, the existence of global poverty may be perfectly acceptable on an ethical level so long as we have not actively caused poverty. Any moral argument that claims we have a duty to reduce poverty lies outside the realm of negative duties and falls, instead, in the realm of positive duties. Pogge recognizes the validity of this logic and therefore utilizes the more concrete framework of negative duties, which require national governments, international organizations, and citizens to refrain from establishing or supporting coercive social institutions that actively harm the world's poor. According to this framework, we can pose the question: have governments, multilateral organizations, and corporations engaged in, or created, structural economic, social, and cultural conditions that constitute a violation of human rights, or a violation of negative rights?

Pogge's general theory is stated as such:

The postulate of a human right to X is tantamount to the demand that, insofar as reasonably possible, any coercive social institutions be so designed that all human beings affected by them have secure access to X. A human right is a moral claim *on* any coercive social institutions imposed upon oneself and therefore a moral claim *against* anyone involved in their imposition.[28]

This construal of a negative rights/duties theory addresses several concerns posed by critics of human rights. First, Pogge's account focuses initially on social institutions in the immediate context of state governments. Resonant with the wording of the Vienna Declaration, which states that the protection of human rights is "the first responsibility of governments," Pogge argues that his framework circumvents one of the main dilemmas of positive rights schemas.[29] Namely, human rights critics argue that the responsibility for the protection of, and the obligation to provide, universal rights, holds everyone accountable to everyone. If we all have an ambiguous positive duty to protect the human rights of all people, then on a certain level the moral responsibility between, say, a landless farmer in a developing country and a wealthy, North American lotto winner is equivalent. In other words, human rights language does not make a clear distinction about whether certain individuals (for example the affluent) have a greater moral imperative to contribute to solving problems of poverty. Although the global poor are still bound by the duty to respect human rights, Pogge's theory centers on the responsibilities of the world's affluent.

Under Pogge's framework, "human rights give you the claims not against all other human beings, but specifically against those who impose a coercive institutional order upon you."[30] Under such a system, participants involved in the creation or maintenance of a social order have a "negative duty" not to cooperate in upholding the system "unless they compensate for their cooperation by protecting its victims or by working for its reform. Those violating this duty share responsibility for the harms, such as insecure access to basic necessities, produced by the unjust institutional order in question."[31] This framework avoids a libertarian formulation of negative duties that runs the risk of disengaging people from social activism on the grounds that we affluent people do not actively create global poverty. Moreover, Pogge's framework also differs from a type of system that holds all accountable to all, namely, the criticism waged against a positive rights framework mentioned above. Ultimately, Pogge's theory holds morally accountable all those who participate in the creation and preservation of socially harmful institutions and social arrangements.

For example, with respect to our analysis of multilateral organizations, Pogge takes issue with the trade liberalization policies of the WTO. If we can demonstrate how WTO policies—or those of any of the multilateral organizations examined in the first three chapters for that matter—impose economic arrangements that harm the global poor, then their policies constitute a violation of human rights. Pogge notes that the problem with the WTO "is not that it opens markets too much, but that it opens *our* markets *too little* and thereby gains for us the benefits of free trade while withholding them from the global poor."[32] The point here is that by withholding benefits from the global poor, wealthy, industrialized countries (such as the United States) are directly sustaining an economic system that constitutes a human rights violation. The final chapter returns to this argument by drawing specific attention to food sovereignty's call for food to be considered a human right, as well as its contention that multilateral (and some developmental) policies constitute what Pogge would consider a violation of human rights.

In sum, Pogge's argument allows us to direct attention to numerous levels of human rights issues and is especially important for our current analysis of food security and food sovereignty. Coupling Pogge's theory of human rights and negative duties with food sovereignty's demand for food to be considered a human right bolsters a critique of the current neoliberal policies of the WTO, the World Bank, and the IMF.

THE CAPABILITIES APPROACH: AMARTYA SEN AND MARTHA NUSSBAUM

Aside from the complex issues associated with human rights, the challenges food sovereignty pose to current economic and developmental models of globalization also invite discussions on theoretical and policy options for addressing global hunger and poverty with respect to human well-being. The following section examines the theory of Amartya Sen and Martha Nussbaum by looking specifically at their respective versions of the capabilities approach. While the capabilities approach does not specifically focus on the demands of food sovereignty, its focus on improving human well-being has a direct connection to how we orient discussions on global poverty, and thus may provide fruitful theoretical and policy ground from which to apply and frame the debate between food security and food sovereignty.

While Sen's and Nussbaum's approaches to global social justice encompass numerous themes pertaining to freedom, equality, and well-being, this section focuses on their respective conceptions of the capabilities approach. The capabilities approach is drawing increased attention in the UN's Human Development Reports as a way to gauge human well-being. However, according to Nussbaum, the United Nations Development Programme's use of capabilities remains essentially rhetorical and, as such, requires more substantive elaboration and implementation.[33] Second, the capabilities approach addresses many of the challenges waged, for example, by critics of the universality of human rights (i.e. the argument from cultural relativism). Both Sen and Nussbaum believe that there needs to be a strong relationship between human rights and capabilities, but their concentration on capabilities in addition to human rights addresses many of the dilemmas we have discussed above. Specifically, Nussbaum's articulation of the capabilities approach is an attempt to substantiate or establish a list of basic human capabilities that could serve as a concrete framework for developing policy. Finally, the capabilities approach introduces themes of economic justice that are the subject of the concluding chapter.

Amartya Sen and Martha Nussbaum have pioneered what is called the capabilities approach to analyzing human development and well-being. For both Sen and Nussbaum, the capabilities approach is a more substantive and fruitful approach to examining global poverty. They both take issue with conventional measures such as GNP per capita or utility because these approaches often obfuscate certain measures of well-being. The GNP per capita measure for example, if taken as the sole indicator for measuring poverty, fails to take certain economic distributions into account and thus proves inadequate for measuring income and wealth inequality. Furthermore, the GNP approach is an inadequate measure of quality of life indicators such as "health, education, gender, and racial justice."[34]

A utilitarian approach to social justice fails on some of the same grounds. Measuring well-being, for example, in terms of abstract measures of happiness, pleasure, or desire—what Sen calls "mental characteristics"—fails to address the important issues of potential well-being. As Nussbaum notes, a utilitarian who "asks people what they currently prefer and how they are, proves inadequate to confront some pressing issues of justice" because people tend to exhibit "adaptive preferences."[35] Adaptive preferences refer to preferences people have adjusted to their immediate social and economic conditions, or in other words, "preferences that adjust to the low level of functioning" people can actually achieve. Nussbaum argues that we are especially likely to encounter examples of adaptive preferences in individuals or groups that have been persistent victims of discrimination. These individuals or groups have internalized their unequal worth and base both their preferences and their standards of well-being on inadequate information about "their situation, their options and the surrounding society."[36] For example, Nussbaum argues that adaptive preferences are especially visible in women in developing countries.

Take for example a mother living in extreme poverty, in conditions in which she cannot provide her children with potable water, sufficient food, education, and so forth. If for whatever reason, say, a foreign aid program manages to provide this mother with enough extra food to keep her children alive, she may express a general increase in happiness (i.e. if we utilize a utilitarian calculus). In other words, she has adapted to her circumstances and conveyed a general increase in net happiness despite the fact that she does not enjoy other basic necessities, much less what we would consider minor joys in life. According to Sen and Nussbaum, this is precisely the sort of phenomenon a utilitarian framework fails to capture. We could also apply this logic to a hypothetical example related to food security. If a rural farmer fails to keep his family farm in operation due to competition with imported goods, but in turn is able to purchase cheaper imported goods—and thus save more income—a utilitarian approach may argue that the farmer's net happiness has increased. Unfortunately, this tells us nothing about how this farmer's condition could have been improved under another economic or social arrangement, namely, an arrangement in which the farmer is able to produce his own food rather than rely on cheap imports.

In *Inequality Reexamined*, Sen poses the question, 'Equality of what?' as a means to introduce the theoretical foundations of the capabilities approach.[37] Examining what we mean when we speak of equality or inequality requires critical examination of the space in which we talk about equality, because the question "equality of what?" is rooted in actual human diversity. Given disparate demands for equality, or "focal variable" upon which we discuss equality or inequality—such as in income, wealth, happiness, liberty, opportunity, rights or need fulfillments—requires clarification. Human diversity, as well as the inherent nature of various focal variables, entails equalities in some spaces that may result in inequalities in other spaces. For example, equality of opportunity can lead to inequality of income, or equality of wealth can coexist with inequality of happiness.[38] This becomes especially important when discussing development and global poverty both in terms of how we conceive of and how we measure global poverty. To understand global poverty simply in terms of income deprivation, while a highly important aspect of the issue, may fail to address what Sen calls the "intrinsic" aspects of poverty. Low income is an instrumental aspect of poverty in the sense that increasing income provides the means to surmounting other aspects of poverty. For example, increasing income may provide greater opportunities for better education and heath care, but it may not adequately identify other factors associated with poverty such as "personal heterogeneities, environmental diversities," and "variations in social climate."[39] For Sen, the capabilities approach expands the field of inquiry to include both the nature and the causes of poverty.

The advantage of the capabilities approach is its ability to measure the well-being of a person in terms of "the quality of the person's being."[40] For Sen, the capabilities approach is grounded in how we conceive of freedom as well as the role freedom plays in the way we organize our social relationships and arrangements. A person's position in a social arrangement can be analyzed on two levels: on the level of actual achievement, and on the level of the freedom to achieve.[41] Actual achievement refers to situations in which humans decide they have a certain goal—say, to generate enough income to purchase a home—and in fact realize this goal (i.e. purchase a home). *Freedom to achieve*, on the other hand, refers to the ability of an individual to actually convert her resources into a specific achievement. Using the above example, the freedom to achieve would mean that the individual with the resources to purchase a home in fact has the freedom to do so. If the individual has the resources, but, say, the government refuses the opportunity for home ownership, then this person lacks the freedom to achieve (i.e. the individual has the resources but does not have the freedom to purchase a home). This distinction is important because it highlights the idea that when examining human well-being we must look not only at what people are able to achieve, but also at the capacity or freedom for people to pursue and achieve their goals.

This distinction between the freedom to achieve and an individual's actual achievements is clarified by Sen's distinction between capabilities and functionings. For Sen, the well-being of a person should be viewed in terms of that person's quality of life, or their "beings and doings."[42] Capability reflects an individual's freedom to "lead one type of life or another."[43] In other words, capability refers to the substantive freedoms people have for choosing the type of life they so desire. Functionings refer to the specific objects or desires a person holds valuable and thus seeks to obtain or achieve. As Sen notes,

Achieved functionings constitute a person's well-being and the "capability to achieve functionings (i.e. all the alternative combinations of functionings a person can chose to have) will constitute the person's freedom—the real opportunities—to have well-being.[44]

If we are to take well-being as the baseline of how we conceive of just social arrangements, we must look at both substantive freedom, or the freedom to choose from a variety of options, and actual achievements, namely, whether individuals are actually able to achieve the combinations of functionings they deem valuable.

Recently Sen has extended the capabilities approach to issues pertaining to global development. In *Development as Freedom*, Sen argues that we should understand global poverty not simply as an issue of low income, but rather, as capability deprivation. By understanding poverty as capability deprivation, we are better equipped to understand complex forms of poverty, as well as to develop effective policy that addresses both income inequality and the overall well-being of people. The final chapter examines Sen's specific rationale for understanding global poverty as capability deprivation, and draws some concrete connections to the debate between food security and food sovereignty. However, before moving on to this discussion, it is important to highlight one of the main distinctions between Sen's and Nussbaum's capability approach.

One of Nussbaum's major criticisms of Sen's version of the capabilities approach is the fact that Sen refrains from offering a substantive list of human capabilities. Nussbaum recognizes that part of Sen's hesitance is due to his emphasis on the concept of freedom, and specifically the freedom of individuals to choose their understanding of well-being. Sen's commitment to freedom appears to be based, in part, on his respect for cultural diversity. Namely, if we want to avoid imposing certain Western ideals on foreign governments and cultures, the capabilities approach must remain somewhat vague so as to allow peoples (and their governments) to decide the best means for securing humans rights and well-being.

While Nussbaum's and Sen's overall commitment to capabilities remains the same, Nussbaum questions Sen's emphasis on freedom as a general social and political goal. Indeed, freedom plays a central role in determining the nature of capabilities as well as the expression of human functioning within an array of possible capabilities, but to simply assert the concept of freedom on an abstract level fails to provide a substantive basis for a political project based on social justice. Remarking on *Development as Freedom*, Nussbaum notes, "Sen speaks throughout the work of 'the perspective of freedom' and uses language, again and again, suggesting that freedom is a general all-purpose social good, and that capabilities are to be seen as instances of this more general good of human freedom." Nussbaum's concern here is the ways in which "some freedoms limit others."[45] As Nussbaum argues, for example,

The freedom of rich people to make large donations to political campaigns limits the equal worth of the right to vote. The freedom of businesses to pollute the environment limits the freedom of citizens to enjoy an unpolluted environment. The freedom of landowners to keep their land limits projects of land reform that might be argued to be central to many freedoms for the poor. And so on.[46]

Nussbaum feels that an abstract concept of freedom fails to provide the foundations for a political project that protects basic liberties and improves the living conditions of the poor. In other words, a meaningful capabilities approach needs to say "forthrightly that some freedoms are central for political purposes, and some are distinctly not."[47]

This is an important point of distinction, because a notion of freedom that is not given concrete expression runs the risk of falling victim to the problems associated with the food security paradigm. Namely, an abstract conception of freedom with respect to particular goals of development may serve to perpetuate current conditions of global poverty. The freedom to pursue profits, to engage in certain trade arrangements, and so forth, may limit the freedoms of the world's poor to pursue different goals (such as the freedom to choose how and what types of foods are produced and consumed).

To address this problematic aspect of Sen's approach, Martha Nussbaum offers a more substantive list of human capabilities, which are paraphrased in the following:

1. Life: The opportunity to live to the end of a normal human life, without premature death or dying "before one's life is so reduced as to not be worth living."
2. Bodily Health: The ability to have good health, including reproductive health, adequate nourishment, and adequate shelter.

3. Bodily Integrity: The ability to move freely from place to place; to be secure against violent assault, including sexual assault and domestic violence; and to have opportunities for sexual satisfaction and choice in matters of reproduction.

4. Senses, Imagination, and Thought: The ability to use the senses—including the ability to imagine, think, and reason—in a "truly human" way, a way informed by an adequate education. The ability to use the imagination in connection with "experiencing and producing expressive works and events of one's own choice, religious, literary, musical, and so forth." The ability to use one's mind in ways that are protected by guarantees of freedom of expression with respect to religious, political and artistic exercises.

5. Emotions: The ability to express human emotions necessary for full human development; this includes the ability to have attachments to things and people outside ourselves; to love, grieve, long, and experience gratitude and justified anger.

6. Practical Reason: The ability to develop one's conception of the good and engage "in critical reflection about the planning of one's life." This involves the protection of liberty of conscious and religious expression.

7. Affiliation.

8. Friendship: The ability to "live for and to others," which includes the ability to recognize and show concern for other humans and to engage in various forms of human interaction. The capability for compassion, justice, and friendship.

9. Respect: "Having the social bases of self-respect and non-humiliation." The ability to be treated as a dignified human being whose worth is equal to that of others. "This entails provisions of non-discrimination on the basis of race, sex, ethnicity, caste, religion, and national origin."

10. Other Species: The ability to live with "concern for and in relation to animals, plants, and the world of nature."

11. Play: The ability to laugh, play, and enjoy recreational activities.

12. Control over one's environment:

13. Political: The ability to participate effectively in political choices that constitute one's life, which includes having the right to political participation and freedom of speech and affiliation.

14. Material: The ability to "hold property (both land and movable goods)." The right to employment, and having freedom from unwarranted search and seizure.[48]

These capabilities, Nussbaum notes, are central *political* goals. Nussbaum's reason for understanding capabilities as goals of public policy is an effort to highlight how capabilities establish the foundations for choice. As she notes, "for political purposes it is appropriate for us to strive for capabilities, and those alone. Citizens must be left free to determine their course after they have these capabilities."[49] The thrust of Nussbaum's argument for capabilities as political goals is the conception of citizens as free and dignified human beings, as makers of choices.[50] Politics play a central role in terms of "providing citizens with the tools that they need, both in order to choose at all and in order to have a realistic option of exercising the most valuable functions."[51] In other words, a capabilities approach not only provides citizens with the freedom to choose their own ends, but also informs citizens about the potential options for choice. Or as Sen puts it, "Political rights are not only important for the fulfillment of needs, they are crucial also for the formulation of needs."[52]

Nussbaum clarifies this point further by making a distinction between "basic," "internal," and "combined capabilities." Briefly stated, basic capabilities refer to the "innate equipment" of individuals that allows for the development of more advanced capabilities. Internal capabilities refer to the conditions necessary for requisite functions. Combined capabilities refer to the "internal capabilities combined with suitable external conditions for the exercise of the function."[53] For example, a person who has access to adequate food, yet chooses to live a life of fasting is still exercising her combined capabilities; namely, she has available food resources, freely chooses to fast, and has the knowledge that there are alternatives to fasting. Alternatively, a woman who is subjected to genital mutilation, whether forcefully or under conditions under which she is unable to make an informed choice, does not have the freedom and capability characteristic of combined capabilities. Again, the exercise of combined capabilities is a political goal. By creating the political conditions necessary for people to choose from a bundle of capabilities, Nussbaum establishes the basic political goals in which we are capable of functioning. Nussbaum contends that this basic list of capabilities is similar to Rawls's notion of primary goods; it represents a list of "opportunities for life-functioning" that every rational person would want. However, "if one ends up having a plan of life that does not make use of all of them, one has hardly been harmed by having the chance to choose a life that does."[54] The emphasis here is a focus on the freedoms people have to decide on the type of life they want, and the beings and doings they deem valuable. Both Sen and Nussbaum recognize that the concept of freedom is a central aspect of the capabilities approach, but Nussbaum is prepared to offer a specific list that can guide policy debate.

CONCLUSION

The final chapter of this study draws some specific connections between the themes of human rights and the capabilities approach with respect to the food security and food sovereignty debate. However, it should be apparent that the analysis of human rights and the capabilities approach highlights some of the central ethical concerns associated with current discussions on globalization and global poverty. As enumerated in the second and third chapters of this project, the criticisms food sovereignty has waged against the multilateral organizations of the World Bank, IMF, and WTO (as well as other actors such as transnational corporations and inept foreign governments) resonate with Pogge's argument that our current global, economic system constitutes a massive violation of human rights, a violation that we as affluent human beings might be implicated in. Fortunately, organizations such as the UN, and developmental theorists such as Amartya Sen and Martha Nussbaum, have made progressive inroads into how we can conceive of global poverty specifically, and global social justice generally, in a way that is hopeful for future theorizing and policy implementation. Drawing off of these themes, the final chapter also offers some concluding remarks on how the demands of food sovereignty can be utilized as conceptual support for understanding humanity, not simply as self-interested, autonomous beings bent on economic gain and profiteering, but rather as communal beings who value the survival of cultural diversity, sustainable development, and the environment.

CHAPTER 5

Ethical Analysis of Food Sovereignty and the Ethics of Globalization

INTRODUCTION

The previous chapter outlined some of the more pressing ethical issues associated with global poverty, concepts of human rights, and positive and negative rights and duties. In response to some of the questions this discussion raised, the capabilities approach of Amartya Sen and Martha Nussbaum was introduced as a fruitful basis from which to potentially realize human rights, as well as a basis from which to conceive of human well-being and flourishing. This chapter continues this discussion by relating these themes specifically to the discussions involved with food security and food sovereignty. Ultimately, the food sovereignty model, and the social movements associated with the general demands of global social justice advocated by food sovereignty, embodies many of the radical proposals advanced by both human rights theory and the capabilities approach. Structurally, the chapter begins with how the food security and food sovereignty debate can be oriented within discussions on human rights. Next, it examines food sovereignty in relation to the capabilities approach, explaining how the capabilities approach resonates with the demands of food sovereignty, as well as how the food sovereignty movement can give specific content to the capabilities approach. Finally, the chapter concludes with some remarks about the challenges the food sovereignty movement faces.

FOOD SECURITY, FOOD SOVEREIGNTY, AND HUMAN RIGHTS

Now that we have outlined some of the central issues associated with the debate between food security and food sovereignty, we can draw some specific connections to the ethical issues associated with human rights. Recall food sovereignty's mission statement outlined in chapter three:

Food sovereignty is the RIGHT of peoples, countries, and state unions to define their agricultural and food policy without the "dumping" of agricultural commodities into foreign countries. Food sovereignty organizes food production and consumption according to the needs of local communities, giving priority to production for local consumption. Food sovereignty includes the right to protect and regulate the national agricultural and livestock production and to shield the domestic market from the dumping of agricultural surpluses and low-price imports from other countries. Landless people, peasants, and small farmers must get access to land, water, and seed as well as productive resources and adequate public services. Food sovereignty and sustainability are a higher priority than trade policies.[1]

Not only does this statement begin with the foundational argument that food should be considered a human right, it also outlines some of the corollary conditions necessary for realizing this right. On an ethical and political level, food sovereignty implicates multiple actors, including individuals, state governments, and multilateral organizations in how we attempt to create more just global food and agriculture systems. To this list we should add entities such as TNCs, given both their influence on state governments and their increasing role in the production, marketing, and distribution of global foods. As such, food sovereignty's mission is broad and inclusive in nature. Its demands require pro-active measures from all peoples and all organizations involved directly or indirectly with the global food system.

On the continuum of developmental and neoliberal conceptions of globalization, the challenge food sovereignty poses to how we think of globalization and poverty in general, and global hunger and malnutrition specifically, represents an indictment of any conception—whether developmental or neoliberal—that does not *actively and successfully* ensure the human right to food. From a developmental perspective, the UN and its subsidiary organizations have made hopeful inroads into expanding human rights first established in the UNDHR. As we saw in the previous chapter, organizations such as UNESCO and covenants such as the ICESCR have expanded how we conceive of cultural and economic rights, and have argued that cultural diversity should play a central role in policy implementation. A respect for human diversity entails a commitment on the part of developmental organizations to recognize how different cultural perspectives can and should contribute to policy formation. With this said, these organizations must continue to discuss the problems associated with human rights and cultural difference. The implementation of human rights may very well differ with respect to country and culture, but with respect to food, the first priority involves drastic efforts to curb hunger and malnutrition. To this extent, the right to food represents a baseline that must be met before cultural disputes over the importance of certain cultural and political rights can be entertained. To state this differently, if people are dying from a lack of food, how can they even participate in a dialogue?

Given the emerging global participation of food sovereignty advocates—from Africa to Europe, Asia, and the Americas—the movement is increasingly representing not just an isolated political-cultural phenomenon, but a worldwide call to re-envision the global politics of food. While food sovereignty calls for specific policy changes, what is also interesting from an ethical perspective is the alternative understanding of the nature of human relations (as well as human flourishing) articulated by the movement. As we saw in chapter three, food sovereignty activists emphasize a radically different concept of humanity, a concept that emphasizes mutual well-being over self-interest, cooperation over competition, the survival of communities, traditions, and cultural values over efficiency and profiteering, and sustainable development over unfettered growth and consumption. With respect to these general themes, the philosophical nature of the movement, on the one hand, reinforces the direction some developmental models of globalization are pursuing, and on the other, serves as a case study upon which ethicists, political scientists, and economists (as well as numerous other players seeking to combat global poverty and hunger) can work in unison to revitalize discussions on human rights and social justice.

Developmental organizations such as the UN have made progress in recognizing the demands of food sovereignty. For example, in an announcement made at the 2008 World Food Summit, the current UN Special Rapporteur, Oliver de Shutter, argued that the current global food production system needs reconfiguration. Smallholder farmers need policies that bolster their capacity to produce locally, and protection from volatile food prices and unfair trade arrangements that prioritize industrialized and heavily subsidized countries. Furthermore, policies must be implemented that strengthen smallholders' ability to negotiate prices with large agri-businesses and that help facilitate more environmentally friendly forms of production. The acknowledgement of these concerns resonates with the impetus behind food sovereignty's mission.[2]

While the UN's efforts are promising, they are not necessarily reason to celebrate. Pogge, for instance, does not hold such an optimistic view of the progress of the UN with respect to curbing global poverty. He argues that a critical examination of the evolution of the UN's Millennium Development Goals reveals that its mission to halve poverty by 2015 remains problematic on several levels. First, Pogge argues that the mission to halve poverty was not new to the MDGs; rather, this endeavor was established at the World Food Summit in Rome in 1996. The first article of the MDGs ostensibly renewed this vision, but with a subtle change in wording. The Rome Declaration spoke of halving the *number* of undernourished people worldwide by 2015, while the first article of the MDGs speaks of halving the *proportion* of undernourished people by 2015.[3] According to Pogge, this substitution of terminology is significant.

For the year 2000, some 1094 million were reported to be living below $1/day. Halving the number of extremely poor people thus would commit us to ensuring that there are no more than 547 million such people in 2015. Halving the proportion of extremely poor people is less ambitious. In 2000, the total human population was about 6070.6 million . . . so 18.02 percent were living in extreme poverty. Halving the proportion means reducing this percentage to 9.01 percent. Given an expected human population of 7197 million in 2015 . . . the implied goal is then to reduce the number of extremely poor people to 648.5 million by 2015. The planned poverty reduction has been shrunk by 101.5 million.[4]

While this technical example calls into question the intent of the MDGs, what should also be highlighted is the need to critically examine how UN documents may appear promising on the surface, but when examined on a more critical economic level, prove otherwise.

On a more philosophical level, Pogge criticizes the MDGs on the basis of their proposed timeline for halving poverty. As outlined in chapter four, Pogge argues that the current world economic order constitutes a violation of human rights on the grounds that affluent countries are actively creating and sustaining a situation in which millions of people die each year due to undernourishment, a lack of safe drinking water, basic sanitation, basic medical care, shelter, and so on. For Pogge, we must ask the question, is halving poverty by 2015 a morally acceptable plan? To answer this, Pogge asks us to consider a hypothetical scenario:

Consider some of the other catastrophes of the last century: the genocide in Rwanda, for example, when the UN and the rest of the world stood idly by while some 800,000 people were hacked to death . . . Suppose some US politician had said, in April 1994, that the genocide in Rwanda is really terrible and that the world's governments should commit themselves to reducing the slaughter by 19 percent by the year 2009. How would this have been received? Or suppose a US politician had said, in 1942, that the German concentration camps are morally intolerable and that the world's governments should aim to achieve a 19-percent reduction in the population of these camps by the year 1957 . . . People would have been absolutely horrified by such a proposal.[5]

The import of this hypothetical consideration is the idea that, given our current resources, technological advances, and ingenuity, we have no moral grounds for such a meager attempt to curb global poverty. With respect to the issue of providing food, for example, both food security and sovereignty models start with the fact that we have the adequate resources to feed the world's poor, yet we not only continue to fail to feed hundreds of millions of people each year, we also fail to take drastic measures to curtail this catastrophe.

The food sovereignty movement draws attention to Pogge's hypothetical comparison in a way that is applicable to the dominant food security model. On a certain level, we may want to applaud the progress made by developmental organizations such as the FAO and IFAD for their successes. However, upon closer inspection, we may also question whether their policies have done enough. For example, as highlighted in chapter one, IFAD's strategy outlined in its 2007–2010 Strategic Framework, despite being a developmental approach that ostensibly takes more consideration of the participation of the agrarian poor with whom it works, remains myopic in its economic approach to development. Natural resources are conceived as a form of capital from which to develop an economic base; microfinance is a potential means for building rural economic infrastructure; agricultural labor is conceived in terms of maximizing growth (rather than as a livelihood); and so forth. Ultimately, both the FAO and IFAD seek to integrate the rural poor into the global market. While these strategies are not inherently bad, they raise important ethical questions. Do the rural poor desire to enter the global marketplace, or would they rather produce local goods for their communities? Do they seek profits in their farming production in the same way large, capital intensive farms do in the United States and Europe? Is the ultimate goal of the agrarian lifestyle one of unfettered production and consumption, or is it more connected to cultural traditions? By seeking ultimately to integrate the rural poor into the world market, developmental organizations such as the FAO and IFAD tacitly conceive of humans in the same way that neoliberals see them, as purely economic beings. The peoples of the food sovereignty movement, on the other hand, fight for an alternative conception of the human being.

These questions become even more poignant when we scrutinize the successes and failures of the neoliberal economic model that drives the theory and policy of the World Bank, IMF, and WTO. As the analysis in the second chapter demonstrated, this record is extremely appalling not only for the global poor, but specifically for the agrarian poor. As we have seen, for example, WTO trade arrangements that privilege industrialized countries, implement asymmetrical, export oriented trade arrangements, and form the architecture of the TRIPS and TRIMS agreements have proven disastrous for many.[6] Moreover, World Bank and IMF loan conditionalities and Structural Adjustment Programs (SAPs) that have historically resulted in governments implementing austerity measures have resulted in the reduction of social safety nets, which creates further hardships for developing countries. Not only do these institutions conceive of human nature solely as *homo economicus,* their policy failures have demonstrated both the inadequacy of this understanding of humanity and the problems associated with global finance and development institutions that function according to this rationale. The food sovereignty movement challenges both the existence of these global governance institutions and their policies precisely on these grounds. Not only have many multilateral policies failed to alleviate the hardships of the world's poor, they have imposed an understanding of human nature radically different from the reality of hundreds of millions of people around the world.

Ultimately, the neoliberal economic model that serves as the driving theoretical framework behind the food security model fails to protect basic human rights. Although food security language has evolved, whether in the language of UN documents or in terms of developmental policy, it is not as radical as the proposals set forth by the food sovereignty movement. In a vein similar to Pogge's understanding of global poverty as a major, ongoing human rights violations, the food sovereignty movement—along with other social justice movements such as the MST, Zapatistas, and Farmer to Farmer movement—represents a revolutionary alternative to both the neoliberal economic understanding of globalization and the global food regime that it has propagated.

The protection of human rights in general, and the right to food in particular, will remain unfulfilled as long as neoliberal economic notions of globalization and human nature continue to dominate theory and policy. Therefore, a more radical approach to human rights needs to be based on an ethic that conceives of our current global food regime as a massive violation of human rights. Accordingly, the peoples of affluent, industrialized countries, and the elite in developing countries, should consider themselves not only complicit in this ongoing violation of human rights, but more forcefully, as active participants in perpetuating current violations. The first step in approaching problems of human rights requires an acknowledgement of our complicity. Once we admit our complicity, we can begin the necessary process of imaginatively and rigorously reformulating policy that can strengthen the force and efficacy of human rights.

In sum, food sovereignty and Pogge's understanding of human rights can work hand in hand. In its foundational claim that food is a human right, the food sovereignty model should incorporate the idea that the current global food system constitutes a violation of human rights. Rather than simply stating that food is a basic human right—a right that includes access to healthy, nutritious, and culturally important foods—food sovereignty should further argue that the failure to provide this basic human right is a violation of human rights. Farmer rights should include the right of consumers to decide what they consume, and how and by whom what they consume is produced. Moreover, agricultural production should focus on local production for local consumption. Agricultural reform must be genuine reform in which landless farmers have greater access to land, water, seeds, and financial mechanisms that allow them to produce for local consumption. Integrating into the global economy should still be an option for small-holder farmers, but this integration should be a choice rather than a necessary evil imposed by policies of the World Bank, IMF, and trade arrangements of the WTO. To this extent, developing countries should be protected from dumping as well as under-priced, imported foods. Finally, agroecological practices that help to ensure the survival of traditional farmer knowledge and create sustainable farmer livelihoods must be given priority. If these basic demands of food sovereignty are not met, the global food regime will remain a violation of human rights.

FOOD SOVEREIGNTY AND THE CAPABILITIES APPROACH: TOWARDS A MORE SUBSTANTIVE UNDERSTANDING OF HUMAN WELL-BEING

The previous chapter examined the capabilities approach pioneered by Martha Nussbaum and Amartya Sen, arguing that it is a fruitful method for conceiving of policy for global poverty. With respect to food sovereignty, however, we must ask whether the capabilities approach and the demands of food sovereignty work hand in hand. And, possibly more importantly, whether the food sovereignty movement informs specific policy proposals for the capabilities approach. The following section provides some potential answers to these questions.

Sen's understanding of poverty as capability deprivation is important on numerous levels. First, the capabilities approach concentrates on "deprivations that are intrinsically important," namely, deprivations other than simply low income.[7] Similar to global poverty measures, such as GDP for instance, which do not adequately measure social inequalities, a measure of well-being solely in terms of income deprivation fails to take into consideration the freedoms people have to use their income in ways that they value. Second, the capabilities approach addresses the relationship between low income and low capability in terms of contextual differences with respect to communities, families, and individuals. By focusing on these differences, the capabilities approach accomplishes several goals. First, the detailed nature of the capabilities approach is more equipped to capture the relationship between income and age, gender, location, epidemiological factors (i.e. diseases endemic to certain regions), and so forth. Second, Sen argues that the capabilities approach captures "conversion" problems associated with income deprivation and the ability to convert income into valued functionings. Handicaps such as age, disability, and illness not only make it difficult for some people to earn an income, they also make it more difficult to convert income into successful functionings. This "coupling" effect is not captured by a simple lowness of income metric. Third, income distribution within the family also raises particular concerns. If, for example, as Sen argues, we find problems with "boy preference" with respect to the distribution of family income—a problem Sen argues is widely manifest in many countries in Asia and North Africa—the income approach does not adequately identify the deprivation of girls. Finally, the capabilities approach is better equipped to address the relationship between relative deprivation in terms of income and absolute deprivation in terms of capabilities. As Sen argues, "Being relatively poor in a rich country can be a great capability handicap, even when one's absolute income is high in terms of world standards."[8] In other words, in a more affluent country an individual needs more income to purchase the goods needed to achieve the same social functioning that she would in a less affluent country. The capabilities approach, with its focus on the social aspects of poverty and deprivation, is better equipped to address these problems.

Nussbaum's notion of human nature and human flourishing can also be an informative framework through which to endorse food sovereignty. The capabilities perspective argues that "a world in which people have all the capabilities on the list is a minimally just and decent world."[9] Establishing the conditions necessary for pursuing the capabilities approach involves tactical strategies in both domestic and international contexts. On a domestic level, the capabilities approach "interprets the purpose of social cooperation as that of establishing principles and institutions that guarantee that all human beings have the capabilities on the list." In other words, Nussbaum's list can serve as a guiding framework for establishing constitutional conditions that ensure basic well-being for a nation's people. In an international context, the outcome oriented nature of the list should be emphasized. Namely, before a nation begins to define who holds certain duties to provide for its citizens, the nation must acknowledge that this list constitutes basic entitlements necessary for a minimally just state.

Nussbaum argues that the capabilities approach focuses on what it means to live a life of dignity. The language of human dignity, as we have seen, is becoming increasingly characteristic of human rights documents of the UN, and, as such, plays an important role in how we define human well-being and human flourishing. Nussbaum argues that "the prerequisites for living a life that is fully human rather than subhuman, a life worthy of the dignity of the human being" must include the need "to live cooperatively with others" and the need to have the capability to "cooperate together for the fulfillment of human needs and the realization of fully human lives." From this basic prerequisite we can determine that a fully human life requires things such as "adequate nutrition, education of the faculties, protection of bodily integrity, liberty for speech and religious self-expression," and so forth.[10] Once we have established these basic perquisites, we can move on to the question of rights and duties, namely, who has the duty to provide these necessities. In part, the elaboration and policy implementation of this task requires the concerted effort of economists, political scientists, and policy-makers. The capabilities approach provides us with a meaningful basis from which to direct policy. For example, the capabilities approach at its heart is an approach that contests the idea of development as economic growth, and instead insists on the idea of human development.[11]

While our discussion of rights has argued that individuals, governments, and institutions are all complicit in failures to produce a more just and humane global order, Nussbaum focuses on the central role institutions play in providing and protecting basic human capabilities. Of specific importance for our present project is the idea that national sovereignty should be respected, albeit "within the constraints of promoting human capabilities."[12] The core element of freedom within the capabilities approach is, in part, proposed as an effort to respect political and cultural diversity, and thus allow states to decide how they choose to provide basic capabilities. It should not be understated, however, that this is not license to disregard the requirements of basic capabilities or the freedoms required for the promotion of them. Instead, it is a means of addressing problems associated, for instance, with the debate between universalism and relativism. Of specific importance here is the idea that transnational corporations also have a responsibility to promote human capabilities within the countries where they do business. This requires a departure from a conventional business ethos of profit maximization to a responsibility to promote good environmental policy, safe and fair labor conditions, education, and so on. Finally, global governance institutions such as the World Bank, IMF, and WTO (along with state governments) must design economic systems that are fair for developing countries. While this list is not exhaustive, it does resonate with the demands of food sovereignty.

Alongside the relationship between institutional responsibilities and the promotion of human rights, the emphasis on freedom and choice inherent to the capabilities approach helps avoid another particular problem associated with the food sovereignty movement. Namely, we must avoid conceiving of the agrarian lifestyle as a sort of romantic, bygone era of simplicity that will inevitably fade away as industrialization presses onward. As food sovereignty advocates have articulated, there is much to be said for a desire to sustain agrarian livelihoods, but in no way is this some sort of pre-modern nostalgia. Instead, and possibly more so than any other current social justice movement, food sovereignty activists understand the need for environmentally safe and sustainable development. Their demand to control the production and consumption of healthy, nutritious, and culturally important foods not only speaks to a system of values, however diverse they may be, but also to a very real concern over current trends in food production and consumption. The burgeoning of genetically modified foods, the monopolization and patenting of seeds and basic grains, and the harmful environmental consequences of capital and chemical intensive farming techniques are rapidly thwarting the ability of farmers to choose how and by whom food is produced and consumed. As we saw with the Monsanto case study, agribusinesses are increasingly consolidating and monopolizing agricultural production, marketing, and distribution. Monsanto is just one example of the corporate power emerging on a global level. As mentioned in chapter two, the top 10 seed companies control 67 percent of the global market share, the top 10 agrochemical company's control 89 percent of the global market share, and the top 10 biotechnology companies control 66 percent of the market share.[13] With this global concentration of agricultural sectors comes the destruction of people's sovereignty

over the production, distribution, and consumption of the foods they desire
and the livelihoods that accompany them.

In contrast to global food networks that privilege large-scale agricultural
production, distribution, and marketing, movements such as the Farmer
to Farmer movement demonstrate people's desire for self-determination,
knowledge generation and sharing, and small-scale, sustainable agriculture. As we saw in chapter three, for example, MCAC's focus on environmentally friendly food production, innovation, solidarity and love of nature,
family, and community represents a radically different conception of development than that of neoliberal concepts of growth and development.
MCAC's gatherings and exchanges, enlivened by food, songs, poems, jokes,
and games, illustrate how their understanding of food production and
agricultural development is inextricably linked to the culture of a community and an agrarian lifestyle. As opposed to a managerial style of knowledge dissemination characteristic of previous neoliberal models, MCAC's
focus is on community-based generation of agricultural knowledge and
experimentation. As we have seen, evidence suggests not only that small-
scale agriculture is more efficient in terms of productivity, but small-scale
production is better equipped to meet the demands of production for local
consumption.

The capabilities approach can serve as a theoretical framework for creating policy to address the demands of agrarian movements, but it can also
be given content by the specific demands of these agrarian movements.
Food sovereignty's petitions for greater control over production processes,
along with fair trade arrangements, greater influence in agrarian policy
formulation, and so forth, provide the capabilities approach some specific
focal points that policy needs to address in order for the agrarian poor to
live lives of dignity and well-being. As such, theorists and policy makers
working within a capabilities paradigm can work in unison to determine
the necessary steps needed for formulating future policy.

CHALLENGES AHEAD FOR FOOD SOVEREIGNTY

In one of the few current critical analyses of the food sovereignty movement, Windfur and Jonsén have identified several major challenges the
movement will encounter in the future. A brief look at these challenges
will contribute to further theory and policy discussions as well as allow us
to make a few remarks on how this current project seeks to contribute to
the effort of food sovereignty.

First, as examined in chapter one, one of the prominent focal points of
the neoliberal macroeconomic model of development and food security is
trade. The food sovereignty model is not against trade in general; rather
it fights for fairer trade arrangements that specifically benefit small-scale
farmers. Global trade arrangements propagated by the WTO have failed

small-scale farmers and created the disastrous conditions the global poor face today. To counter the WTO's failures, food sovereignty argues that countries and farmer groups should have the option of restricting trade if it proves detrimental to small-holders. This demand may come in the form of more adequate trade arrangements—arrangements that developed countries such as the United States and Europe actually abide by—or in the more radical demand by groups such as *La Via Campesina* for the WTO to stay out of agriculture.[14]

Second, many developmental policies created during the Green Revolution (i.e. genetically modified seeds, advanced agricultural technologies, capital intensive inputs, etc.) were implemented with the hopes of providing greater yields, which many believed would help generate food resources adequate for a growing global population. Although these policies have proven to be somewhat insufficient, food sovereignty must show how small-scale farming and agroecology are proper alternatives to Green Revolution tactics. As we saw in chapter three, evidence does in fact suggest that small-scale farming is more productive than these tactics. Part of the ethical argument presented in this and the previous chapter is that the values embodied by food sovereignty are values that need respecting. This is not to suggest that the food sovereignty model is insufficient for curbing global hunger, but rather that it is up to policy makers to continue experimenting with ways to meet the demands of food sovereignty.[15]

Third, the language of sovereignty may also prove problematic. With the rising power of multilateral organizations and TNCs, many theorists have questioned the effective power of state governments. Currently the food sovereignty model emphasizes the political will of state governments, rather than the demand that the peoples directly affected by policy, the distribution of resources, and national and international decision-making process, have control over these processes.[16] As mentioned above, one possible way of accomplishing this goal is to make global governance institutions more democratic in nature. However, it should be noted that debate will continue as to whether the entire structure of global governance is legitimate. If food sovereignty's demands of local production for local use are ultimately realized, this may entail the dismantling of global governance institutions.

Finally, food sovereignty must elaborate upon its articulation of human rights. As it stands currently, its concept of human rights is still vague in nature. It does not specify exactly who has the obligation to provide the right to food or the right to have control over production processes. Although it does argue that individuals, communities, and states should have control over how food is produced, distributed, marketed, and consumed, food sovereignty advocates will need to continue to elaborate how sovereignty over these processes takes place. Moreover, state governments must be provided a larger policy space in which to secure food for their peoples.[17] State governments must also be committed to fighting for the interests of the small-scale, peasant, and landless producers. On an international level, food sovereignty will therefore need to continue to elaborate the status of food as a human right, clarifying, for example, whether food constitutes a legal, economic, or cultural right, or all three.

Pogge's ethical argument—that our current global order constitutes a massive violation of human rights—offers a potentially fruitful framework from which food sovereignty can articulate the human right to food. Namely, the fact that food security, as it is conceived and implemented through neoliberal models of globalization, has failed to substantially curb global hunger is grounds to question whether this model contributes to a global food regime that constitutes a violation of human rights. Given that we have the capacity to feed the world's poor, even if simply on a basic caloric level, begs the question: have we done enough? Neoliberal models of globalization, models that emphasize notions of competition, individuality, and profiteering—with attending policies of unfettered growth and consumption, trade liberalization, privatization, deregulation, and so forth—have proven disastrous for much of the global poor. As one aspect of global poverty, therefore, the food security model embedded in the World Bank, IMF, and WTO policies and trade arrangements certainly constitutes a violation of human rights. Moreover, despite the fact that UN organizations have made progress with respect to understanding the demands of food sovereignty, they too have failed to implement policy that lessens the impoverishment of nearly one billion people each year. Pogge's theory helps us to conceptualize the human right to food in a more rigorous and ethically demanding fashion. Coupling a negative rights/duties approach to human rights with the capabilities approach provides both a theoretical and pragmatic paradigm from which food sovereignty may move forward in the future.

FOOD SOVEREIGNTY'S CHALLENGE TO *HOMO ECONOMICUS*

Alongside this ongoing debate on the relationship between food security, food sovereignty, and human rights, food sovereignty also represents a drastically different understanding of human relationships. Although it would be inaccurate to suggest that food sovereignty is fundamentally anti-globalization in nature, it does symbolize a clear alternative to a purely economic understanding of human relations—both human-to-human relationships and our relationship to the natural environment—that is characteristic of a neoliberal conception of humanity. One avenue of future research should focus on the normative nature of economic theory. The idea that economics is not a pure or hard science is not new, and many economists have emphasized the normative nature of the discipline.[18] Theorists who understand economics as a normative discipline—or at least argue that economics has a strong ethical nature—choose to ask questions that relate the science of economics to the ethics of economics. In other words, they approach the discipline by asking: Does economic theory represent reality? Should economic theory not only attempt to describe reality, but also help us envision and create a better world?

Although the food sovereignty model is not directly concerned with exploring new economic theories, themes such as sustainable development, environmental conservation, and pro-poor growth are topics within economics that are garnering renewed interest. As Goodwin notes,

The elite in academic economics supported the economic/political elite in providing the theoretical basis for the global spread of neoliberalism. The 'Washington Consensus' was a bundle of ideas that justified the imposition of the neoliberal financial, trading, and small-government regime on the less developed nations of the world. The increasingly well-documented failures of this approach have been used in the global revolt against globalization and its theoretic underpinnings, which sets the stage for economics in the twenty-first century.[19]

The fact that neoliberal economic policies have failed with respect to problems such as curbing global poverty has created more fodder for economists who challenge theoretical notions of perfect markets, perfect competition, perfect knowledge, and perfect rationality. These foundational assumptions not only fail to represent reality, but serve as the basis of ineffective neoliberal policy.[20]

Goodwin also argues that neoliberal economic theory is entrenched in a particular concept of efficiency, which in turn is directly linked to a particular understanding of consumption. Efficiency is about getting more of everything, consumption is equated with utility (or what we all value/ desire), and therefore the goal of economics is and should be the maximization of consumption. Obviously this is partly true. We need consumption (and the desire to consume) for an economy to function, but we should also ask how the economic drive to consume differs in developing versus affluent countries. In developing countries, consumption may be the primary economic goal given a lack of natural and capital resources. Alternatively, consumption in more affluent countries may be an economic goal simply to keep the economic wheels turning.[21] In other words, we people in developed countries should continue to ask: is more always better?

The ways in which the food sovereignty movement explicitly or implicitly challenges conventional neoliberal economic theory is also demonstrated in terms of gender justice, an integral aspect of social justice groups such as food sovereignty, the MST, and the Zapatistas. Economist Bina Agarwal, for example, shows how conventional economic models based primarily on simple notions of altruism or self-interest may not apply to inter-household relationships. Instead of the notion that households are homogeneous economic entities that are run by an altruistic patriarch, household relationships are often characterized by a mixture of conflict and cooperation.[22] The interests of women within the household are not necessarily in accord with the male family members, and, as such, their interests may be radically different. For example, some researchers argue that women are more inclined to look after family or community needs (especially with respect to children) before or instead of personal gain.[23] In developing countries, women often allocate income in ways that ensure the health and well-being of their families before their personal well-being, suggesting to a certain extent that women may embody a more altruistic rationale than their male counterparts. Altruistic behavior depends on the specific context, but what is important is the fact that basing policy and economic models that simply understand humans as autonomous, self-interested beings is not always adequate. By challenging this usually-male understanding of economic behavior, food sovereignty activists embody another crucial point of contention with current understandings of globalization.

Food sovereignty draws attention to the integral role women play, not only in micro-economies such as the household, but also in larger economic contexts. Unfortunately, the track record is not great, as women continue to face discrimination. Although women comprise half of the world's population, they receive only a small portion of its benefits and opportunities.[24] They face constant struggle against cultural marginalization, they face political opposition to get jobs, and they are often denied access to basic education.[25] As such, women are often shackled by the duel challenge of caring for the household and extra-household constraints on their efforts to achieve well-being. Food sovereignty's emphasis on the unacknowledged economic role of impoverished women is another pivotal platform on which it can press forward with its cause.

What is important here is the potential for new social movements, such as food sovereignty, to provide further support for and justification of non-neoliberal schools of economic thought. Rather than stubbornly insisting that economics is value neutral—an insistence especially characteristic of neoliberal economics—we should start with the fact that economics is indeed normative, and thus should play a central role in how we go about making the world more just. To this extent, food sovereignty may draw from what Goodwin calls "heterodox economics"—schools such as feminist, ecological, social, and political economics—in an effort to augment food sovereignty's overall challenge to neoliberal globalization.

FOOD SOVEREIGNTY AND DEMOCRACY

As we have seen, a major advantage of the capabilities approach is the fact that it focuses on the choices individuals can make. An individual's capabilities are constituted by any particular bundle of functionings he or she deems valuable. Accordingly, as Sen emphasizes, part of measuring well-being also involves determining the extent to which individuals are able to convert their capabilities into valued functionings. Although the capabilities approach has made progress in this respect, future research will need to incorporate a more substantive analysis of how social power, and specifically institutionalized power, plays a major factor in determining the extent to which individuals are able to convert capabilities into valued functionings.[26]

For example, Sen argues that democratic institutions, with attending civil liberties, are a necessary prerequisite for achieving basic human freedoms and well-being. Although we have already covered some of the problems associated with the distinction between first order human rights (civil and political rights) and second order social and economic rights, this does not mean that basic political liberties and rights should be adumbrated in the process of providing basic human necessities. As a social institution, Sen argues democracy has "intrinsic," "instrumental," and "constructive" importance with respect to development and poverty reduction. Democracy has intrinsic importance for the realization of basic capabilities to the extent that political and social participation is a desired goal of most peoples.[27] Democracy has instrumental and constructive importance to the extent that argumentation, public debate, and open communication help people to form ideas of what they want. To effectively understand what sorts of economic needs people are able to articulate requires discussion and exchange of ideas. Moreover, under a democratic regime, political leaders, if they desire to remain in power, are more likely to listen to the demands of the people.[28]

While Sen's understanding of the importance of democracy pertains broadly to the achievement of basic capabilities, his discussion can be of specific relevance to the food sovereignty movement. First and foremost, we can apply this discussion to the structure of multilateral organizations such as the IMF and World Bank. Joseph Stiglitz argues the IMF is a prime example of the undemocratic nature of these institutions. For example, the IMF is accountable to a full-time board of directors, who in turn are accountable to governments, who in turn are theoretically accountable to the people. However, as Stiglitz notes:

[O]ne has to recognize how frail these links are. The executive directors are accountable not so much to the governments themselves as to particular agencies within those governments. To be sure, these agencies are accountable to the government, and the government—at least in democracies—is accountable to the people . . . The IMF responds more to those to whom it is directly accountable than to whom it ultimately ought to be responsible. Its governors are finance-ministers and central bank governors, and they represent a specific segment of society. Their interests are very different from those of labor ministers. The whole culture of the IMF would be different if it was accountable to different agencies within the government.[29]

The sheer length of the chain of accountability thus makes it virtually impossible for the people affected by failed IMF policies to seek recourse. People may resort to not reelecting their government officials who agreed to IMF programs during their office, but in essence IMF officials remain relatively immune and thus unaccountable. The problem of accountability is only one aspect of the undemocratic nature of the IMF. Stiglitz argues that a more problematic aspect of the structure of the IMF is its voting structure. Currently, voting shares within the IMF are in proportion to an "outdated and imperfectly measured economic weight," in which the wealthiest countries have more voting power, and thus determine what policies—usually those that benefit the wealthy countries—are pursued.[30]

Stiglitz notes that the representational structure of the World Bank is more accountable than the IMF insofar as the World Bank has to answer to more governmental bodies, including environmental, education, and health ministers. As such, the World Bank receives a broader input of perspectives on how different policies will impact various demographics within particular countries. However, this should not be a cause for celebration. Despite recognition by the World Bank, IMF, and WTO that some of their previous developmental policies failed or proved detrimental to the global poor, these organizations still remain largely committed to the idea of neoliberal global governance. In other words, the structure of global governance is not questioned.

In the short term, continuing efforts to democratize these multilateral organizations is imperative for food sovereignty advocates. With that said, if democratizing these organizations proves antithetical to their very structure, it may be time to reconsider whether global governance is needed in the future. The central problem of democratizing is, again, an issue of accountability. In reality, small-scale farmers have to first mobilize behind a democratic candidate who prioritizes their interests, and second, gain a legitimate voice in determining policy within these multilateral organizations. This may be an unrealistic goal. For example, this is currently evident by the fact that food sovereignty advocates have called for the WTO to stay out of agriculture. Unfortunately, given the aforementioned problems with democratic decision making, the movement has yet to see any substantive change in WTO trade arrangements. This was evident in the July 2008 failure to come to an agreement with respect to the Doha round of trade discussions.[31]

However, the food sovereignty movement is making inroads through protest and advancing alternative visions of globalization. As we saw in the case study on the MST in chapter three, for example, landless Brazilian farmers have challenged neoliberal-based land reform not only through legal channels (by constitutionally challenging large, rural landowners' right to fallow land), but also through the assertion of a completely different style of life, namely a livelihood that emphasizes democratic decision making within their settlements. With respect to agricultural reform, the MST has focused on land production for local and family use, whether through land ownership arrangements whereby property is owned individually but labor and production are engaged collectively, or through labor and work done on collectively owned land. Regardless of the particular land ownership arrangement, the MST represents a radical alternative to market based agricultural reform. As Martins argues:

Rural landowners oppose cooperative forms of possession, production, and work. They seem aware that these experiences can escalate from the local to the national sphere and may consolidate new practices of social organization and political participation that could undermine private property rights. In this context, to make a massive and radical proposal for agrarian reform is not simply to call for land redistribution to incorporate more farmers into the capitalist system; rather, it necessarily involves shifting the entire agrarian structure of production, power, and cultural relations. This means that the whole economic-social-political system would have to be changed.[32]

The MST movement represents one such expression of the challenge the food sovereignty movement presents to both developmental and neoliberal models of food security and market-based agricultural reform. Not only does it seek more equitable land reform and land usage, but on a more philosophical level the movement challenges the notion of human relations characteristic of the neoliberal economic model. As a larger social movement, the MST also embodies some of the same issues with respect to social power that could aid in advancing the implementation of the capabilities approach.

If members of social and political justice movements such as the MST, the Zapatistas, and the Farmer to Farmer movement continue to exemplify values of gender equality, democratic decision making, and sustainable and environmentally safe development, they will continue to be powerful examples of change. While these social justice movements are mostly located in developing countries, there are ways in which we citizens of affluent countries can aid their efforts. The following two case studies on the Slow Food movement and fair trade exemplify two options for social activism against the fast-paced lifestyle and destructive global trade arrangements that harm millions around the world.

THE SLOW FOOD MOVEMENT CASE STUDY: A PRACTICE FOR APPLYING ETHICAL EATING

The Slow Food Movement was officially established as an international organization and movement in 1989 as an alternative to fast-paced life, specifically with respect to our eating habits, our knowledge of how food is produced, where it comes from, and how it affects the natural environment.[33] As its mission statement states, Slow Food seeks to "counteract fast food and fast life, the disappearance of local food traditions and people's dwindling interest in the food they eat, where it comes from, how it tastes and how our food choices affect the rest of the world."[34] The Slow Food Movement centers on the concepts of "co-producers," the international exchange of knowledge, and sustainable agriculture. Understanding ourselves as co-producers rather than consumers involves "taking interest in those that produce our food, how they produce it and the problems they face in doing so."[35] An international exchange of knowledge with respect to food production provides avenues in which we can educate ourselves about where our food comes from, how it is produced, who produces it, and the availability of healthy, flavorful, and traditional cuisines.

Because Slow Food attempts to counter the current drive towards the standardization, industrialization, and homogenization of food, it is also strongly linked to what it terms "new agriculture," agricultural methods that focus on sustainability, biodiversity, and the preservation, improvement, and spreading of traditional knowledge. The Slow Food Movement is a relatively new movement that seeks to draw off of many academic disciplines and social movements to advance the struggle against harmful aspects of globalization. Utilizing what it calls the "science of gastronomy," the Slow Food Movement is emerging as an endeavor to both scientifically and ethically challenge our current global food system. For example, from a natural science disciplinary perspective, Slow Food activists draw from genetics and botany to study and catalogue seed varieties in an effort to research current seed diversity, as well as future directions for protecting and cultivating seed diversity. The movement draws from chemistry in an effort to restore foods natural, original flavor and to study traditional techniques of preservation and processing (as opposed to artificial flavoring and chemical-intensive methods of processing and preservation). It draws from agroecology in its effort to understand where our food comes from and how to produce it in the most ecologically friendly manner, a manner in which the livelihoods of global farmers are protected and promoted.[36]

As we have seen, one of the central themes of food sovereignty is its dedication to local rather than global relationships between producers and consumers. Slow Food's notion of producers and co-producers resonates well with this idea to the extent that Slow Food organizations attempt, on the one hand, to rhetorically link consumers to the production process. By considering ourselves co-producers, we have a greater stake in the production process and thus may re-envision our relationship to the foods we consume. On the other hand, the Slow Food Movement is more than rhetoric because it implicates us all in ethical and political relationships of responsibility. It requires us to learn where the foods we eat come from, how the foods we eat affect, positively or negatively, those who produce them, and how the foods we eat impact the natural environment. As Pretty notes, "The most political act we do on a daily basis is to eat, as our actions affect farms, landscapes and food businesses."[37] To this extent, local food can be understood as a political and ethical act of resistance to current global models of food production that are based on homogenization, standardization, and questionable health quality. As a political-ethical act, eating also challenges us to reconceptualize what it means to be human. As Petrini argues,

Food is the primary defining factor of human identity, because what we eat is always a cultural product. If we accept the existence of a conceptual juxtaposition between nature and culture (between what is natural and what is artificial), food is the result of a series of processes (cultural ones, because they introduce artificial elements into the naturalness of things) that transform it from a completely natural base (the raw material) into the product of a culture (what we eat).[38]

While Petrini's insistence of food as the defining factor of human identity is perhaps stated strongly, it does draw attention to a foundational theme of food sovereignty, namely, the idea that food is not only a basic human necessity, but also an expression of cultural differences, human relationships, and how people understand the natural world.

The Slow Food Movement embodies another example of contemporary social activism that challenges a purely economic notion of globalization and human relations. While Slow Food does not focus explicitly on the link between food production and consumption and global poverty, it does offer another way to approach how we understand food from an ethical and political standpoint. It provides us not only with an alternative theoretical framework for understanding our relationship between what we eat and those who produce our foods, but also with practices we can engage in to achieve a more sustainable and conscientious mode of consumption. For example, Petrini offers a list of things Americans can do to strengthen our food communities:

1. Join a local Slow Food convivium.
2. Trace your food sources.
3. Shop at a local farmers' market.
4. Join a CSA (Community-Supported Agriculture).
5. Invite a friend over for a meal.
6. Visit a farm in your area.
7. Create a new food memory for a child. Let the child plant seeds or harvest greens for a meal.
8. Start a kitchen garden.
9. Learn your local food history. Find a food that is celebrated as being originally from or best grown/produced in your part of the country.

While this list is not a panacea for global hunger and malnutrition, it does offer concrete practices we can employ to begin making our current global food regime more just.

Although Slow Food represents one current way to re-envision our global food regime, it is not the only movement through which people can participate in a more ethically and politically responsible mode of food consumption. Initiatives such as Fair Trade and organizations such as Community-Supported Agriculture (CSA) are two further examples. Fair Trade initiatives are another means to more firmly connect producers and consumers by ensuring that the goods purchased are goods traded in agreements that directly benefit the farmers who produce them. CSA is founded on binding agreements between farmers and consumers that serve to share the risks and rewards of food production; in other words, a more transparent food economy. CSA also raises awareness about the realities behind food production, as well as constitutes a space in which people can "focus on community, value-sharing, and the celebration of interdependence."[39] Fair Trade and CSA are additional practices that can potentially serve to create a more just global food regime.

Ultimately the Slow Food Movement, as well as other forms of food related social activism such as Fair Trade and CSA, reinforces a larger ethical theme that is visible in contemporary social movements that protest current forms of globalization. These forms of activism do not urge us to become anti-globalization activists per se, but rather invite us to imagine a more ethical global food system. The Slow Food Movement does not propose that we eat only foods that are specific to our own cultural context; in fact, activists argue the opposite, namely, that we are missing out on all sorts of nutritious, flavorful, and naturally sustainable types of food—as well as the rich cultural traditions behind them—by settling for standardized and homogenized foods. Although Slow Food, Fair Trade, and CSA serve as three examples of social and political activism, they are part and parcel of the overall ethical choice food sovereignty presents us. By engaging in social activism that aids in the struggles of food sovereignty, we make small steps toward realizing a more just global food system.

CASE STUDY: FAIR TRADE AND CHALLENGES FOR FOOD RELATED SOCIAL JUSTICE MOVEMENTS

The Fair Trade Movement is another means by which food rights activists can join in global social movements that challenge the destructive forces of the WTO's unbalanced trade policies and the corporate monopolization of the global food system. Rooted in the basic desire to establish trade relations based on respect for human dignity, cultural diversity, and the creation of opportunities for economically and socially marginalized producers, Fair Trade is a producer/consumer practice that can potentially help food sovereignty realize its goals.[40]

Dating back to the 1960s, the Fair Trade Movement grew out of numerous European initiatives that sought more equitable North/South trade arrangements. Supporters of Fair Trade recognize injustice in the current world economy, and see unfair trade arrangements as yet another example of worker and farmer exploitation. To confront these injustices, Fair Trade, much like the Slow Food Movement, seeks to create stronger connections between consumers and producers. Creating these solidarity links works both ways. Producers are able to improve their economic conditions, and consumers gain a greater awareness of where their products come from, the conditions in which their products are produced, and the impact overconsumption has on the wider world. As Laura Raynolds points out, "By building new consumer/producer solidarity links, fair trade seeks to re-embed the production and marketing of major agricultural and non-agricultural exports from countries of the South in more equitable social relations."[41] However, as the Fair Trade Federation notes, Fair Trade is "not about charity," but rather about creating trade relationships that empower producers and help build the economic infrastructure of developing countries. Moreover, Fair Trade reinforces the belief on both sides of the producer/consumer chain that the livelihoods of the world's farmers should be respected and valued.

Currently, Fair Trade standards are determined largely through the Fairtrade Labelling Organization International (FLO). This nongovernmental organization was created with the goal of harmonizing a labeling system for products produced under fair production and trade conditions. With three major Fair Trade labels (TransFair, Max Havelaar, and Fairtrade Mark) under its auspices, the FLO has created Fair Trade principles and procedures for products such as coffee, bananas, tea, cocoa, sugar, honey, and orange juice.[42] Part of the uniqueness about Fair Trade standards is the conditions producers must meet in order to earn the Fair Trade label. Generally, the certification process takes about six months and involves visits by FLO monitors to production sites. FLO monitors also make yearly visits to ensure that basic social and environmental thresholds are met. To receive the Fair Trade label, producers must be a democratically structured organization of smallgrowers or plantations where workers have adequate representation in production decision making processes. The FLO also requires Fair Trade producers to make a concerted effort to protect forests and wildlife habitat, prevent soil erosion and water pollution, and reduce the usage of chemically intensive fertilizers and pesticides. Fair Trade producers must also abide by labor standards, including the right to association and collective bargaining, freedom from workplace discrimination, and the right to safe and healthy work conditions. And, finally, trade relations must be aimed as much as possible toward long-term agreements.[43] By structuring agreements with the long-term in mind, Fair Trade arrangements seek to produce a greater level of employment security for farmers and producers.

Fair Trade offers an alternative to harmful conventional trade arrangements that asymmetrically benefit wealthy, Northern countries. To date, the success of Fair Trade partnerships continues to increase. According to the World Trade Fair Organization, there are currently "over a million small-scale producers and workers are organized in as many as 3,000 grassroots organizations and their umbrella structures in over 50 countries in the South"[44] As of 2006, Fair Trade sales worldwide had surpassed U.S. $2.6 billion, and Fair Trade agreements had provided approximately five million people (800,000 households) a decent living.[45] Fair Trade practices hold enormous potential for hunger and poverty reduction as well. Take for example Oxfam International's estimates of bolstering trade in developing regions:

If Africa, East Asia, South Asia, and Latin America were each to increase their share of world exports by one per cent, the resulting gains in income could lift 128 million people out of poverty. In Africa alone, this would generate $70 billion—approximately five times what the continent receives in aid.[46]

The potential for Fair Trade to unlock these fallow resources highlights the ongoing need for food rights activists to engage in, and inform the public about, Fair Trade causes.

Accomplishing Fair Trade goals is inextricably connected to the same themes food sovereignty activists struggle against. IMF conditionalities that force developing countries to open their markets to global trade fail to see how these conditions harm the world's poor. Instead, Fair Trade arrangements that protect small-scale producers can mitigate the often difficult and harmful transition into larger global markets. Moreover, Fair Trade challenges WTO trade arrangements that unfairly benefit industrialized countries by forcing developing countries to dismantle domestic food production protections. Fair Trade also calls for the elimination of all forms of dumping, a tactic that we have already seen to be extremely harmful to global farmers.

Although Fair Trade has great potential, as consumers we must also be aware of the potential for it to become vulnerable to corporate takeover. As Raynolds notes, "there is also a risk that the space that exists for alternative trade will be subverted by profit seeking corporations . . . corporations [that] are trying to bolster their legitimacy by adopting the rhetoric of environmental and/or social responsibility." In fact, these practices are "little more than a corporate facelift."[47] Fair Trade advocates worry that, as Fair Trade becomes more popular, large corporations will realize the potential profit of this industry and attempt to move in. The corporatization of Fair Trade would eventually lead to the same problems inherent to massive agribusinesses, namely where profit and incentive based business models become the norm. However, "To avoid being absorbed by corporations and their conventional trade practices, alternative trade movements must build new and tighter links between Southern producers and Northern consumers."[48] While corporate takeover has not occurred to date, Fair Trade consumers must be proactive in terms of scrutinizing where their products come from and under what conditions they are produced.

In the short-term, Fair Trade also faces the pragmatic problem of higher prices. Because Fair Trade goods still circulate in niche markets and must compete with underpriced, subsidized goods, their prices are naturally higher than the mass produced farm products available to consumers. However, the ultimate goal of establishing a more just global trading system is to inform consumers of the "social and environmental conditions under which commodities are produced."[49] We consumers in affluent countries might have to pay a slightly higher price for Fair Trade products, but perhaps this is an ethical opportunity to start protesting unfair global trade arrangements. Whether we buy Fair Trade coffee beans from southern Mexico or bananas from Jamaica, small consumer decisions are a good starting point for becoming active in the global struggle against hunger and malnutrition.

CONCLUSION

The juxtaposition of the food security model, as it is manifest in multilateral organizations such as the World Bank, IMF, WTO, and United Nations, and the emerging concept and movement of food sovereignty, reveals crucial ethical issues pertinent to global hunger and malnutrition. On a larger scale, the issues associated with the global food system are central to our understanding of globalization and poverty. Within the food sovereignty movement, myriad social, political, and economic justice movements such as the MST, Zapatista, Farmer to Farmer, Fair Trade, and Slow Food Movements have also begun to challenge and resist the harmful consequences of neoliberal globalization. Ultimately, what becomes clear is that the dominant food security model is still guided primarily by neoliberal economic theory that conceives of humans as *homo economicus*—beings guided principally by individuality, the pursuit of single-minded self-interest, competition, and profiteering. Alternatively, food sovereignty and its supporters embody an alternative to the philosophical underpinnings of neoliberalism insofar as they understand human nature in terms of social interdependence, cooperation, community building, and respect for nature and its resources. Food sovereignty presents us all with an ethical choice, a choice that invariably challenges both how we see the world and what we think constitutes a just world.

Although developmental economic theory and policy have made progress in terms of establishing global food security, in many ways they remain entrenched in the philosophical underpinnings of neoliberal economic thought. The food security model has failed both on its own terms with respect to its goal to feed the world's hungry and malnourished, and with respect to the radicality of its goals. Given our technological advances, massive gaps between rich and poor, and viable choices to curb poverty, we should unobjectionably demand answers for why we continue to allow over 840 million people go hungry each year, and over one billion people to live below the poverty line. The food security model has proven unable to answer these questions. On top of this basic shortcoming, the food security model fails to adequately address and respect the ways in which agrarian livelihoods are meaningful to the world's small-scale, peasant, and landless farmers. This failure is part and parcel of a dominant neoliberal model of globalization that divides humanity, destroys lives and the environment, and insists that this is a desirable state of affairs.

Although issues associated with globalization, global poverty, and hunger and malnutrition are complicated, neoliberal theory and policy has failed to create a more just global order and thus needs to be changed. In part, this failure is due to the fact that neoliberalism does not represent the lived reality of the majority of the world's people. This project has focused specifically on the issue of food security as one manifestation of this failure.

Fighting to eliminate hunger is one step in the overall process of challenging neoliberal globalization. If we can move beyond a food security model, which focuses primarily on securing adequate caloric intake for the world's hungry and malnourished, and towards a model that simultaneously curbs hunger and protects the cultural traditions inherent in food, we allow ourselves to envision new forms of globalization that respect cultural diversity and the traditions associated with food, rural farming, and community life.

The food sovereignty movement represents an alternative that provides us with this opportunity. Admittedly, the movement still faces challenges, both in terms of clarifying its overall goals and in terms of establishing a clear and viable policy platform from which to advance its cause. This book has sought to aid in this effort primarily through applying a more radical notion of human rights and by suggesting that the capabilities approach is the most fruitful approach to achieve the goals of food sovereignty.

Notes

INTRODUCTION

1. Miguel A Altieri, "Food Price Increases—Who Gets Hurt and What Can Be Done About It," *FoodFirst*, April 11, 2008, http://www.foodfirst.org/en/node/2084 (accessed January 6, 2008).

2. Joseph Stiglitz presents a compelling description of how the World Bank and IMF have evolved since their inception after WWII. The IMF was originally created to provide global macroeconomic stability, while the World Bank was to provide structural stability, namely, how governments spent their money. It was always the purpose of the World Bank to address issues of poverty, but eventually the IMF got on board as well. See Joseph Stiglitz, *Globalization and its Discontents* (New York: W. W. Norton & Company, 2003), 195.

3. Will Petrik, "COHA's Analysis of the IMF and IDB Part 1," *The Guatemala Times*, April 23, 2009, http://www.guatemala-times.com/news/world/1047-cohaas-analysis-of-the-imf-and-the-idb-part-1.html (accessed July 1, 2009).

4. Amartya Sen, "The Idea of Justice," *Journal of Human Development* 9, no. 3 (November 2008): 337.

5. United Nations, "Declaration of Human Rights," http://un.org/Overview/rights.html#a6 (accessed December 17, 2008).

6. Martha Nussbaum, "Capabilities and Human Rights," *Fordham Law Review* 66 (1997): 283.

CHAPTER 1

1. United Nations Economic and Social Council, "Economic, Social and Cultural Rights: The Right to Food," February 9, 2004, E/CN.4/2004/10, http://www.unhchr.ch/huridocda/huridoca.nsf/(Symbol)/E.CN.4.2004.10.En (accessed December 17, 2008), 4.

2. Olivier De Schutter, Report of the Special Rapporteur on the Right to Food, July 21, 2009, http://www2.ohchr.org/english/bodies/hrcouncil/docs/12 session/A-HRC-12-31.pdf (accessed October 9, 2009).

3. Amy L. Staples, *The Birth of Development: How the World Bank, Food and Agriculture Organization, and World Health Organization Changed the World, 1945–1965* (Kent, OH: The Kent State University Press, 2006), 34.

4. Ibid., 37.

5. Joseph E. Stiglitz, *Globalization and its Discontents* (New York: W. W. Norton & Company, 2003), 23.

6. As Stiglitz demonstrates, the IMF was originally founded on the Keynesian economic assumption that markets do in fact experience failures, and, as such, need government intervention to mitigate market failures.

7. Stiglitz, *Globalization and its Discontents*, 14.

8. Staples, *The Birth of Development*, 87.

9. United Nations Development Program (UNDP), "Millennium Development Goals: A Compact Among Nations to End Human Poverty," *Human Development Report 2003* (New York: Oxford University Press, 2003), v. For a good discussion of the MDGs see Jeffrey Sachs, *The End of Poverty: Economic Possibilities for Our Time* (New York: Penguin Books, 2005). While Sachs is concerned about the failure to reach many of the benchmarks of the MDGs, he remains optimistic. His criticisms focus primarily on the failure of industrialized governments (such as the U.S. government) to live up to their promised donor aid as well as some unsuccessful economic strategies initiated by organizations such as the IMF. Overall, however, he does not challenge the existence of global governance institutions such as the IMF, WTO, and World Bank. For a stronger criticism of these organizations see Joseph E. Stiglitz's *Globalization and its Discontents*. Again, while Stiglitz is more condemning of institutions such as the IMF, he does not go as far as to challenge the concept of such organizations.

10. Sachs, *The End of Poverty*, 80.

11. IFAD, "About IFAD," http://www.ifad.org/governance/index.htm (accessed January 15, 2009).

12. Ibid.

13. IFAD, "A Summary of IFAD's Strategic Framework 2007–2010," http://www.ifad.org/governance/index.htm. (accessed January 15, 2009), 6–7.

14. IFAD, "Rural Finance: From Unsustainable Projects to Sustainable Institutions for the Poor,"http://www.ifad.org/pub/other/rural_e.pdf., 5 (accessed January 15, 2009).

15. It is outside the focus of this section to delve into a discussion on programs that focus on donors or food for aid programs. What is important here is how organizations such as IFAD advocate certain programs (such as MFIs) that encourage self-sustainability and economic growth.

16. IFAD, "Rural Finance: From Unsustainable Projects to Sustainable Institutions for the Poor," 11 (accessed February 15, 2008).

17. IFAD, "IFAD Strategy for Knowledge Management," http://www.ifad.org/gbdocs/eb/90/e/EB-2007-90-R-4.pdf., 8 (accessed February 15, 2008).

18. Ibid., 1.

19. Ibid., 3.

20. FAO, "The State of Food Insecurity in the World 2006," http://www.fao.org/docrep/009/a0750e/a0750e00.htm, 6 (accessed April 3, 2009).

21. Ibid., 6.

22. Ibid., 30–31.

23. WTO, "What is the WTO?" http://www.wto.org/english/thewto_e/whatis_e/whatis_e.htm (accessed January 2, 2008).

24. WTO, "Ministerial Declaration" WT/MIN(01)/DEC/1, 2001, 1 http://www.wto.org/english/thewto_e/minist_e/min01_e/min01_e.htm (accessed January 2, 2008).

25. Ibid.

26. WTO, "Ten Benefits of the WTO Trading System," http://www.wto.org/english/thewto_e/whatis_e/10ben_e/10b00_e.htm (accessed January 2, 2008).

27. WTO, "The Doha Development Agenda," http://www.wto.org/english/thewto_e/whatis_e/whatis_e.htm (accessed January 2, 2008).

28. WTO, "Ministerial Declaration," 3.

29. WTO, "Domestic Support in Agriculture: The Boxes," http://www.wto.org/english/tratop_e/agric_e/agboxes_e.htm.

30. WTO, "Ministerial Declaration," 4.

31. WTO, "Understanding the WTO: The Agreements. Intellectual Property: Protection and Enforcement," http://www.wto.org/english/thewto_e/whatis_e/tif_e /agrm7_e.htm (accessed January 2, 2008).

32. WTO, (2007f), "WTO Programme on Aid-for-Trade," WT/AFT/W/26, http://www.wto.org/english/tratop_e/devel_e/a4t_e/aid4trade_e.htm (accessed January 2, 2008).

33. Ibid.

34. Ibid.

35. FAO, "FAO Tells WTO Meeting that Trade Liberalization Can Promote Food Security," http://www.fao.org/newsroom/en/news/2005/1000191/index.html (accessed April 3, 2008).

36. Ibid.

37. FAO, "The State of Food Insecurity in the World 2006," http://www.fao.org/docrep/009/a0750e/a0750e00.htm (accessed April 3, 2008).

38. Walden Bello, *Dark Victory: The United States and Global Poverty* (Oakland: Food First Books, 1994), 36.

39. The World Bank, "Reaching the Rural Poor: A Renewed Strategy for Rural Development," (Washington, D.C.: 2002).

40. Ibid., 6–7.

41. Ibid., 8.

42. Ibid., 9.

43. Ibid., 10.

44. Ibid., 11.

45. Ibid., 14.

46. Ibid., 15.

47. The World Bank. "World Development Report 2008: Agriculture for Development," (Washington, D.C.: 2008).

48. Ibid., 1.

49. Ibid., 3.

50. Ibid., 3.

51. Ibid., 4.

52. Ibid., 4.

53. Ibid., 5.

54. Ibid., 9.

55. Ibid., 9.

56. Ibid., 10.

57. IMF, "IMF Surveillance," http://www.imf.org/external/np/exr/facts/surv.htm (accessed February 15, 2008).

58. IMF, "IMF Lending," http://www.imf.org/external/np/exr/facts/howlend.htm (accessed February 15, 2008).

59. IMF, "Technical Assistance," http://www.imf.org/external/np/exr/facts/tech.htm (accessed February 15, 2008).

60. Ibid.

61. IMF, "IMF Discusses Market Access for Developing Country Exports," http://www.imf.org/external/np/sec/pn/2002/pn02110.htm (accessed February 15, 2008).

62. International Monetary Fund and the World Bank, "Doha Development Agenda and Aid for Trade," http://www.imf.org/external/np/pp/eng/2005/091905.pdf (accessed March 4, 2009).

63. Philip McMichael, *Development and Social Change: A Global Perspective* 2nd ed. (Thousand Oaks, CA: Pine Forge Press, 2000), 59.

64. Harriet Friedmann, "The International Political Economy of Food: A Global Crisis," in *Food in the USA: A Reader,* ed. Carele Counihan, 326 (New York: Routledge, 2002).

65. Ibid., 327.

66. Ibid., 328.

67. Ibid., 328.

68. Ibid., 329.

69. Ibid., 332.

70. Harriet Friedmann, "Remaking 'Traditions': How We Eat, What We Eat and the Changing Political Economy of Food," in *Women Working the NAFTA Food Chain: Women, Food and Globalization,* ed. by Deborah Barndt, 35–60 (Toronto: Sumach Press, 1999).

71. McMichael, *Development and Social Change: A Global Perspective,* 126.

72. Ibid., 128.

73. For example see Jeffrey Sachs's discussion of "clinical economics" in *The End of Poverty.*

CHAPTER 2

1. IFAD, "IFAD Strategy for Knowledge Management," http://www.ifad.org/gbdocs/eb/90/e/EB-2007-90-R-4.pdf, vi (accessed February 15, 2008).

2. Karol Boudreaux and Tyler Cowen. "The Micromagic of Microcredit." *Wilson Quarterly* 32, no. 1 (Winter 2008): 29. Boudreaux also demonstrates that microloans tend to have high interest rates compared to what we are used to in industrialized countries. These rates may be as high as 50 to 100 percent. However, Boudreaux also notes that these rates are still much lower than the rates these people might incur if they were to borrow from local money lenders.

3. Ibid.

4. IFAD, "Rural Finance: From Unsustainable Projects to Sustainable Institutions for the Poor," http://www.ifad.org/pub/other/rural_e.pdf (accessed February 15, 2008): 5.

5. Vandana Shiva, "Shiva Responds to the Grameen Bank." *Synthesis/Regeneration* 17 (1998), http://www.greens.org/s-r/17/17-15.html (accessed January 25, 2008).

6. Vandana Shiva, "Microcredit: Solution to Poverty or False 'Compassionate Capitalism?'" *Democracy Now,* December 12, 2006.

7. Ibid.

8. FAO, "The State of Food and Agriculture 1996," http://www.fao.org/docrep/003/w1358e/w1358e00.htm (accessed April 3, 2008).

9. Cynthia Moe-Lobeda, *Healing a Broken World: Globalization and God* (Minneapolis: Fortress Press, 2002), 58.

10. FAO, "FAO Tells WTO Meeting that Trade Liberalization Can Promote Food Security," http://www.fao.org/newsroom/en/news/2005/1000191/index.html (accessed April 3, 2008).

11. Quoted in Peter Rosset, "The U.S. Opposes the Right to Food at World Summit," http://www.mindfully.org/Food/Right-To-Food30jun02.htm (accessed March 4, 2009).

12. Quoted in Peter Rosset, "The U.S. Opposes Right to Food at World Summit," *Food First,* June 30, 2002. http://www.foodfirst.org/archive/media/opeds/2002/usopposes.html (accessed February 27, 2008).

13. Graham Hancock, *Lords of Poverty: The Power, Prestige, and Corruption of the International Aid Business* (New York: The Atlantic Monthly Press, 1989), 168.

14. Frances Moore Lappé, Joseph Collins, and Peter Rosset. *World Hunger: 12 Myths* (New York: Grove Press, 1998).

15. Ibid., 132.

16. Michael Maren, *The Road to Hell: The Ravaging Effects of Foreign Aid and International Charity* (New York: The Free Press, 1997).

17. Hancock, *Lords of Poverty,* 13–14.

18. Ibid., 19.

19. Peter Rosset, Raj Patel, and Michael Courville, *Promised Land: Competing Visions of Agrarian Reform* (Oakland, CA: Food First Books, 2006), 18–24.

20. Ibid., 28–29.

21. Vandana Shiva, "War Against Nature and the People of the South," in *Views from the South: The Effects of Globalization and the WTO on Third World Countries,* ed. Sarah Anderson, 91–125 (Oakland, CA: Food First Books, 2000).

22. It is also interesting to note Monsanto's political and lobby influence within the U.S. government. According to the PANNA organization's corporate profile, Monsanto donated U.S. $390,703 to federal candidates from 1994 to 2002, the majority of which went to Republican candidates. It also gave U.S. $1.3 million in soft money donations in 2002 along with Monsanto employee direct donations totaling U.S. $465,141. From 1998 to 2004 Monsanto spent U.S. $22,504,610 lobbying the federal government. See PANNA, Corporate Profile: Monsanto Company, http://www.panna.org/resources/caia/corpProfilesMonsanto (accessed January 17, 2008).

23. Vandana Shiva, "War Against Nature and the People of the South."

24. Hope Shand, "Intellectual Property: Enhancing Corporate Monopoly and Bioserfdom," in *The Fatal Harvest Reader: The Tragedy of Industrial Agriculture,* ed. Andrew Kimbrell, 240–48 (Washington: Island Press, 2002).

25. Nancy Birdsall and John Nellis, "Winners and Losers: Assessing the Distributional Impact of Privatization," *World Development* 31, no. 10 (October 2003): 1617–33.

26. Joseph E. Stiglitz, "Democratizing the International Monetary Fund and the World Bank: Governance and Accountability," *Governance: An International Journal of Policy, Administration, and Institutions* 16, no. 1. (February 2003): 125.

27. The World Bank, "Reaching the Rural Poor: A Renewed Strategy for Rural Development," (Washington, D.C.: 2002), 14.

28. Raj Patel, "Critical Themes in Agrarian Reform," in *Promised Land: Competing Visions of Agrarian Reform*, ed. Peter Rosset, Raj Patel, and Michael Courville, 95–98 (Oakland: Food First Books, 2006).

29. Saturnino M. Borras Jr., "The Underlying Assumptions, Theory and Practice of Neoliberal Land Policies," in *Promised Land: Competing Visions of Agrarian Reform*, eds. Peter Rosset, Raj Patel, and Michael Courville, 99–128 (Oakland, CA: Food First Books, 2006).

30. Klaus Deininger and Hans Binswanger, "The Evolution of the World Bank's Land Policy," in *Access to Land, Rural Poverty, and Public Action*, ed. Alain De Janvry, Gustavo Gordillo, and Jean-Philippe Platteau (Oxford: Oxford University Press, 2001), 408.

31. Borras, "The Underlying Assumptions, Theory, and Practice of Neoliberal Land Policies," 116–17.

32. Mark Weisbrot, Dean Baker, Robert Naiman, and Gila Neta, "Growth May Be Good for the Poor—But are IMF and World Bank Policies Good for Growth?" Center for Economic and Policy Research, http://www.cepr.net/index.php?option=com_content&task=view&id=427 (accessed February 15, 2008)

33. Walden Bello, *Dark Victory: The United States and Global Poverty* (Oakland, CA: Food First Books, 1994), 37–42.

34. Enrique C. Ochoa, *Feeding Mexico: The Political Uses of Food since 1910* (Wilmington, DE: Scholarly Resources Books, 2000), 208.

35. Ibid., 39.

36. Ibid., 40.

37. David Lind and Elizabeth Barham. "The Social Life of the Tortilla: Food, Cultural Politics, and Contested Commodification," *Agriculture and Human Values* 21 (2004): 9.

38. Ibid., 9.

39. Ibid., 10.

40. Anthony De Palma, "How a Tortilla Empire Was Built on Favoritism," *The New York Times*, February 15, 1996.

41. Ibid.

42. Ibid., 10.

43. Raj Patel and Gisele Henriques, "Agricultural Trade Liberalization and Mexico," *Food First Policy Brief No. 7* (Oakland, CA: Food First Institute for Food and Development Policy, 2003), 31. Patel and Henriques attribute this price increase to two factors. On one hand, following the dismantling of government subsidization of tortilla prices for consumers (through the CONASUPO program) and coupled with market liberalization in 1996, tortilla manufacturers were able to transfer costs to customers. On the other hand, the current Mexican tortilla market is monopolized by the two largest companies, GIMSA and MINSA, which respectively control 70 percent and 27 percent of output.

44. Ibid., 10.

45. Luis Hernández Navarro, "The New Tortilla War," *Americas Program Special Report* (Silver City, NM: International Relations Center, May 7, 2007).

46. Ibid.

47. Edward T. Pound and Danielle Knight, "Cleaning up the World Bank," *U.S. News and World Report*, March 26, 2006, http://www.usnews.com/usnews/biztech/articles/060403/3worldbank.htm (accessed February 11, 2008).

48. Government Accountability Project (GAP), "Corruption Exposed at World Bank," March 27, 2006, http://www.whistleblower.org/content/press_detail.cfm?press_id=408 (accessed February 11, 2008).

49. Pound and Knight, "Cleaning up the World Bank," 3.

50. Joseph E. Stiglitz, *Globalization and its Discontents* (New York: W.W. Norton & Company, 2003), 226–27.

51. Ibid., 242.

52. Ibid., 12.

53. Ibid., 55.

54. Ibid., 59.

55. Cairn Smaller, "Planting the Rights Seed: A Human Rights Perspective on Agriculture Trade and the WTO," Institute for Agriculture and Trade Policy, *Backgrounder* no. 1 (Minneapolis, MN: 2005).

56. Organic Consumers Association, "Monsanto's Government Ties," http://www.organicconsumers.org/monlink.cfm#monsanto (accessed January 22, 2008).

57. Andrew Kimbrell and Joseph Mendelson, "Monsanto vs. U.S. Farmers: A Report by the Center for Food Safety," (Washington, D.C.: The Center for Food Safety, 2005), 4. Also available at http://www.centerforfoodsafety.org/Monsantovsusfarmersreport.cfm

58. Kimbrell and Mendelson, "Monsanto vs. U.S. Farmers," 8–9.

59. Ibid., 10.

60. Ibid., 17.

61. CBC News, "Percy Schmeiser's Battle," May 21, 2001, http://www.cbc.ca/news/background/genetics_modification/percyschmeiser.html (accessed 27 February 2008).

62. Paul Elias and Anne Fitzgerald, "Monsanto Sues Farmer Customers over Piracy Issues," *Des Moines Register* January 30, 2005, http://www.mindfully.org/GE/2005/Monsanto-Sues-Farmers30jan05.htm (February 27, 2008).

63. Stiglitz, *Globalization and its Discontents*, 195.

64. Kevin Danaher, *Ten Reasons to Abolish the IMF and World Bank*, 2nd ed. (New York: Seven Stories Press, 2001).

65. Philip McMichael, "The Power of Food," *Agriculture and Human Values* 17 (2000): 1.

66. Harriet Friedmann, "Remaking 'Traditions': How We Eat, What We Eat and the Changing Political Economy of Food," in *Women Working the NAFTA Food Chain: Women, Food and Globalization*, ed. Deborah Barndt, (Toronto: Sumach Press, 1999), 35–60.

67. Bill Prichard and Robert Fagan, "Circuits of Capital and Transnational Corporate Spatial Behaviour: Nestle in Southeast Asia," *International Journal of Sociology of Agriculture and Food* 8 (1999): 3–20. For a good literature review of analytical themes pertaining to food and globalization, see Lynne Phillips, "Food and Globalization," *Annual Review of Anthropology* vol. 35 (2006): 37–57.

68. William D. Heffernanand Douglas H. Constance, "Transnational Corporations and the Globalization of the Food System," in *From Columbus to Con Agra: The Globalization of Agriculture and Food*, ed., Alessandro Bonanno et al., 29–51 (Lawrence: University of Kansas Press, 1994), 29.

69. Philip McMichael, "Global Development and the Corporate Food Regime," in *New Directions in the Sociology of Global Development*, ed. Fredrick H. Buttel and Philip McMichael (Oxford: Elsevier, 2005). In relation to Heffernan and Constance, McMichael does not restrict the analysis of the question of what the driving force

behind the restructuring of the global food system is simply to TNCs. While Mc-Michael does recognize the growing influence of powerful agribusinesses, he considers them as one organizing agent within the greater matrix of global governing regimes (multilaterals) (WTO, World Bank and IMF) and nation states.

70. Ibid., 1.

71. Ibid., 2.

72. Ibid., 5.

CHAPTER 3

1. La Via Campesina, "The International Peasant's Voice," http://www.viacam pesina.org/main_en/index.php?option=com_content&task=blogcategory&id=27&Itemid=44 (accessed March 13, 2008).

2. Ibid.

3. Peter Rosset, "The Multiple Functions and Benefits of Small Farm Agriculture: In the Context of Global Trade Negotiations," *Food First Policy Brief No. 4.* (Oakland: Food First Institute for Food and Development Policy, 1999).

4. Ibid., 1.

5. Ibid., 5.

6. Ibid., 10.

7. Miguel A. Altieri, "Agroecology: The Science of Natural Resource Management for Poor Farmers in Marginal Environments." *Agriculture, Ecosystems & Environment* 93, no. 9 (December 2002): 8.

8. Ibid.

9. Miguel A. Altieri, Peter Rosset, and Ann Thrupp, "The Potential Of Agroecology to Combat Hunger in the Developing World," *Policy Brief No. 55.* (Washington, D.C.: IFPRI, 1998).

10. Vandana Shiva, ed. *Manifestos on the Future of Food and Seed* (Cambridge, MA: South End Press, 2007), 77.

11. Erosion, Technology and Concentration Action Group (ETC), "Who Owns Nature? Corporate Power and the Final Frontier in the Commodification of Life," no. 100 (November 2008), http://www.etcgroup.org/en/materials/publications.html?pub_id=706 (accessed December 17, 2008).

12. Vandana Shiva, *Stolen Harvest: The Hijacking of the Global Food Supply* (Cambridge, MA: South End Press, 2000), 80.

13. Juana Curio, "Seed at the Center of Food Sovereignty," *Seed Heritage of the People for the Good of Humanity* 10, http://viacampesina.org/main_en/images/stories/pdf/seed_heritage_of_the_people_for_the_good_of_humanity.pdf (accessed May 21, 2008).

14. Ibid., 12.

15. Manpreet Sethi, "Land Reform in India: Issues and Challenges," in *Promised Land: Competing Visions of Agrarian Reform,* ed., Peter Rosset, Raj Patel, and Michael Courville, 73–94 (Oakland, CA: Food First Books, 2006), 89.

16. Tom Hayden, *The Zapatista Reader* (New York: Thunder's Mouth Press, 2002), 6.

17. George A. Collier and Elizabeth Quaratiello, *Basta!: Land and the Zapatista Rebellion in Chiapas,* 3rd ed. (Oakland, CA: Food First Books, 2005), 2.

18. Sixth Declaration of the Selva Lacandona, http://www.anarkismo.net/newswire.php?story_id=805 (accessed February 10, 2009).

19. Neil Harvey, "Rebellion in Chiapas: Rural Reforms and Popular Struggle," *Third World Quarterly* 16, no. 1 (March 1995): 43.

20. Ibid., 44.

21. Ibid., 45.

22. Collier and Quaratiello, *Basta!*, 166–67.

23. Cory Fisher-Hoffman, Tessa Landreau-Brasmuck, Kaya Weidman, and Mandy Skinner, "The First Zapatista Women's Encuentro: A Collective Voice Of Resistance," (January 24, 2008), http://www.viacampesina.org/main_en/index.php?option=com_content&task=view&id=479&Itemid=39 (accessed May 28, 2008).

24. See for example Karol Boudreaux and Tyler Cowen, "The Micromagic of Microcredit," *Wilson Quarterly* 32, no. 1 (Winter 2008), 27–31.

25. Jerry Mander, "Machine Logic: Industrializing Nature and Agriculture," in *The Fatal Harvest Reader: The Tragedy of Industrial Agriculture,* ed. Andrew Kimbrell, 87–91 (Island Press: Foundation for Deep Ecology, 2002), 88.

26. Alice Waters, "The Ethics of Eating: Why Environmentalism Starts at the Breakfast Table," in *The Fatal Harvest Reader: The Tragedy of Industrial Agriculture,* ed. Andrew Kimbrell (Washington, D.C.: Island Press, 2002) , 283–87.

27. Eric Holt-Giménez, *Campesino a Campesino: Voices from Latin America's Farmer to Farmer Movement for Sustainable Agriculture* (Oakland, CA: Food First Books, 2006), 78.

28. Ibid., 104.

29. Eric Holt-Giménez, "The Campesino a Campesino Movement: Farmer-led, Sustainable Agriculture in Central American and Mexico," in *The Paradox of Plenty: Hunger in a Bountiful World,* ed. by Doglas Boucher, 297–314 (Oakland, CA: Food First Books, 1999).

30. Holt-Giménez, *Campesino a Campesino,* 89.

31. Ibid., 91.

32. Ibid., 92.

33. Erosion, Technology and Concentration Action Group (ETC Group), "The World's Top Ten Seed Companies—2006," http://www.etcgroup.org/en/materials/publications.html?pub_id=656 (accessed April 3, 2008).

34. Eric Holt-Giménez, "The Biofuel Myths," *International Herald Tribune,* July 10, 2007, http://www.foodfirst.org/node/1716 (accessed March 17, 2008).

35. Ibid.

36. Ibid.

37. United States, "Fact Sheet: Energy Independence and Security Act of 2007," http://georgewbush-whitehouse.archives.gov/news/releases/2007/12/20071219-1.html (accessed February 21, 2009).

38. Eric Holt-Giménez, "U.S.-based Coalition Call for a Moratorium on U.S. Incentives for Biofuels," *Food First,* http://www.foodfirst.org/node/1811 (accessed March 17, 2008).

39. Hamza Hasan, "Overview of U.S. Ethanol Market." Food First/Institute for Food and Development Policy, http://www.foodfirst.org/node/1723 (accessed March 17, 2008).

40. Laura Carlsen, "The Agrofuels Trap," *Americas Program Special Report,* September 11, 2007, http://americas.irc-online.org/am/4535 (accessed March 17, 2008).

41. Victor Quintana, "Biofuels and Small Farmers," America's Program, http://americas.irc-online.org/am/4510 (accessed February 10, 2009).

42. MST (Brazil's Landless Worker Movement), "About the MST," http://www.mstbrazil.org/?q=about (accessed April 14, 2008). See also Angus Wright and Wendy Wolford, "Now is the Time: The MST and Grassroots Land Reform in Brazil," *Food First Backgrounder* 9, no. 2 (Spring 2003).

43. MST, "About the MST."

44. Mônica Dias Martins, "Learning to Participate: The MST Experience in Brazil," in *Promised Land: Competing Visions of Agrarian Reform*, ed. Peter Rosset, Raj Patel, and Michael Courville (Oakland, CA: Food First Books, 2006), 272.

45. MST, "Sectors and Collectives: How the MST Organizes Its Work, Gender Sector," http://www.mstbrazil.org/?q=about (accessed April 14, 2008).

46. Ibid.

47. See Mark S. Langevin, and Peter Rosset, "Land Reform from Below: The Landless Workers Movement in Brazil," in *The Paradox of Plenty: Hunger in a Bountiful World*, ed. Douglas Boucher, 323–29 (Oakland, CA: Food First Books, 1999).

48. Michael Windfuhr and Jennie Jonsén. *Food Sovereignty: Towards Democracy in Localised Food Systems* (United Kingdom: ITDG Publishing, 2005), 6.

49. Ibid., 13.

50. Rebecca Spector, "Fully Integrated Food Systems: Regaining Connections between Farmers and Consumers," In *The Fatal Harvest Reader: The Tragedy of Industrial Agriculture*, ed. Andrew Kimbrel, 288–94 (Washington: Island Press, 2002), 289.

51. Raj Patel, *Stuffed and Starved: The Hidden Battle for the World Food System* (Brooklyn, NY: Melville House Publishing, 2007), 203.

CHAPTER 4

1. Martha Nussbaum, "Capabilities as Fundamental Entitlements: Sen and Social Justice," *Feminist Economics* 9, no. 2 (July 2003): 37.

2. David Selby, *Human Rights* (Cambridge, MA: Cambridge University Press, 1987), 12.

3. United Nations, "Declaration of Human Rights," http://un.org/Overview/rights.html#a6 (accessed December 17, 2008).

4. While it is outside the purview of this project to examine multiple theories of cultural relativism, it should be noted that moral relativism is often distinguished from cultural relativism. Moral relativism holds that we cannot establish universal *moral* or *ethical* norms, while cultural relativism is a more descriptive notion that holds that cultural difference limits an individual's ability to fully understand a culture different than one's own. However, with respect to the analysis of relativism in this section, the overall critique of universalism remains applicable in the sense that critiques of human rights challenge the idea that we can establish a system of norms, rules, rights, and so forth that apply to every individual regardless of cultural or moral differences. For a good example of these issues see Alison Rentlen, "Relativism and the Search for Human Rights," *American Anthropologist* 90, no. 1 (March 1988): 56–72. Rentlen notes that both critics and proponents of relativism have somewhat missed the thrust of relativism. As a descriptive theory, relativism can aid in founding ideas of tolerance, but it would be a mistake to assume that, as such, it also necessarily leads to ethical or moral relativism. In other words, ethical or moral relativism is a subset of the more descriptive/empirical notion of cultural relativism, and thus deserves a different method of analysis. See also Burns H. Weston, "The Universality of Human Rights in a Multicultured

World," in *Human Rights in the World Community: Issues and Action* 3rd ed., ed. Richard Pierre Claude and Burns H. Weston (Philadelphia: University of Pennsylvania Press, 2006). For another good critique of human rights and relativism see Andreas Follesdal, "Human Rights and Relativism," in *Real World Justice*, eds. Andreas Follesdal and Thomas Pogge (The Netherlands: Springer, 2005), 265–83. For various perspectives on the debate between "East Asian" values and "Western" values, see Joanne R. Bauer and Daniel A. Bell eds., *The East Asian Challenge for Human Rights* (Cambridge: Cambridge University Press, 1999).

5. United Nations, "Universal Declaration of Human Rights." For a good discussion of themes presented in this section, see Massimo Ivanoe "The Universality of Human Rights and the International Protection of Cultural Diversity: Some Theoretical and Practical Considerations," *International Journal on Minority and Group Rights* 14 (2007): 231–62.

6. The ethical analysis in this section does not challenge the philosophical premises of the UN's rights language founded upon human dignity, but rather moves directly to the theoretical and pragmatic issues surrounding what types of rights we are examining and the implementation and protection of these human rights.

7. UNESCO, "Declaration on Cultural Diversity," (Paris, France: 2001). Also available at: http://unesdoc.unesco.org/images/0012/001271/127160m.pdf.

8. Ibid., article 1.

9. Ibid., article 2.

10. Ibid., article 3.

11. Ibid., article 5.

12. United Nations, "Vienna Declaration and Programme of Action," (Vienna: June 14–25, 1993).

13. UN, "Declaration of Human Rights," article 27.

14. "International Covenant on Economic, Social and Cultural Rights," article 13.

15. Ibid., article 15.

16. Glen A. Dower, *International Cooperation for Social Justice: Global and Regional Protection of Economic/Social Rights* (Westport, CT: Greenwood Press, 1985), 21.

17. Ibid., 22.

18. Mary Dowell-Jones, *Contextualizing the International Covenant on Economic, Social and Cultural Rights: Assessing the Economic Deficit* (Leiden/Boston: Martinus Nijhoff Publishers, 2004), 2.

19. Rajeev Patel, Radhika Balakrishnan, and Uma Nayaran, "Explorations on Human Rights," *Feminist Economics* 13, no.1 (January 2007): 92.

20. Alan Gerwith, *The Community of Rights* (Chicago: University of Chicago Press, 1996), 54–62.

21. Ibid., 55.

22. Peter Singer, "Famine, Affluence, and Morality," *Philosophy and Public Affairs* 1, no. 3 (Spring 1972): 231.

23. Thomas Pogge, *World Poverty and Human Rights* (Malden, MA: Blackwell Publishers, 2002), 29.

24. Thomas Pogge, "A Cosmopolitan Perspective on the Global Economic Order," in *The Political Philosophy of Cosmopolitanism*, ed. Gillian Brock and Harry Brighouse, 92–109 (Cambridge: Cambridge University Press, 2005), 96.

25. Ibid., 96.

26. Pogge, *World Poverty and Human Rights*, 13.

27. Pablo Gilabert, "The Duty to Eradicate Global Poverty: Positive or Negative?" *Ethical Theory and Moral Practice* 7, no. 5 (November 2004): 538.

28. Pogge, *World Poverty and Human Rights*, 46.

29. It should be noted, however, that Pogge is somewhat critical of the United Nations. See for example his criticism of the Millennium Development Goals in "The First UN Millennium Development Goal: A Cause for Celebration?" in *Real World Justice*, eds. Andreas Follesdal and Thomas Pogge, 317–39 (The Netherlands: Springer, 2005).

30. Pogge, *World Poverty and Human Rights*, 67.

31. Ibid., 67.

32. Ibid., 19.

33. Martha Nussbaum, "Capabilities as Fundamental Entitlements: Sen and Social Justice," *Feminist Economics* 9, no. 2 (July 2003): 35.

34. Martha Nussbaum, "Poverty and Human Functioning: Capabilities as Fundamental Entitlements," in *Poverty and Inequality*, ed. David B. Grusky and Ravi Kanbur, 47–75 (Stanford, CA: Stanford University Press, 2006), 47.

35. Ibid., 48. See also Martha Nussbaum, "Capabilities and Human Rights," 283.

36. Nussbaum, "Capabilities and Human Rights," 283.

37. Amartya Sen, *Inequality Reexamined* (Cambridge, MA: Harvard University Press, 1992), ix. Sen also asks the question 'why equality?' which will not be examined here. Suffice to say, theories that might take the opposite approach by arguing against equality on the grounds that people are fundamentally unequal (depending on what one is examining), and thus, may need to be treated unequally, still end up making claims about equality—which is the thrust of Sen's analysis.

38. Ibid., 2.

39. Amartya Sen, *Development as Freedom* (New York: Anchor Books, 1999), 109.

40. Sen, *Inequality Reexamined*, 39.

41. Ibid., 31–38.

42. Ibid., 39.

43. Ibid., 40.

44. Ibid., 40.

45. Nussbaum, "Poverty and Human Functioning," 62.

46. Ibid., 62.

47. Ibid., 62.

48. Nussbaum, "Capabilities and Human Rights," 287–88.

49. Ibid., 289.

50. Ibid., 292.

51. Ibid., 292.

52. Ibid., 291.

53. Ibid., 290.

54. Ibid., 290.

CHAPTER 5

1. La Via Campesina, "The International Peasant's Voice," http://www.viacampesina.org/main_en/index.php?option=com_content&task=blogcategory&id=27&Itemid=44 (accessed March 13, 2008).

2. Oliver De Shutter, "New Production System Needed To Tackle Global Food Crisis, Says UN Expert," *United Nations Press Release 16* (October 2008), http://

www.unhchr.ch/huricane/huricane.nsf/view01/E196DCEE1E94E39DC12574 E4002FC6CA?opendocument (accessed December 17, 2008).

3. Thomas Pogge, "The First UN Millennium Development Goal: A Cause for Celebration?" in *Real World Justice,* ed. Andreas Follesdal and Thomas Pogge, 317–38 (The Netherlands: Springer, 2005), 318.

4. Ibid., 318.

5. Ibid., 329.

6. See Peter Rosset, *Food is Different: Why We Must Get the WTO Out of Agriculture* (Nova Scotia: Fernwood Publishing, 2006).

7. Amartya Sen, *Development as Freedom* (New York: Anchor Books, 1999), 87.

8. Ibid., 88–89.

9. Martha Nussbaum, "Beyond the Social Contract," in *The Political Philosophy of Cosmopolitanism,* ed. Gillian Brock and Harry Brighouse, 196–218 (Cambridge: Cambridge University Press, 2005), 210.

10. Ibid., 210.

11. Ibid., 212.

12. Ibid, 215.

13. Erosion, Technology and Concentration Action Group. "Who Owns Nature? Corporate Power and the Final Frontier in the Commodification of Life," no. 100 (November 2008), http://www.etcgroup.org/en/materials/publications. html?pub_id=706 (accessed December, 17 2008): 4.

14. Michael Windfuhr and Jennie Jonsén, *Food Sovereignty: Towards Democracy in Localised Food Systems* (United Kingdom: ITDG Publishing, 2005), 31.

15. Ibid., 32.

16. Ibid., 33.

17. For a good discussion of the relationship between food security and the need for increased policy space for state governments, see Kumar Nagesh and Kevin Gallagher, "Relevance of 'Policy Space' for Development: Implications for Multilateral Trade Negotiations," *Research and Information System for Developing Countries* no. 120 (New Delhi: India, 2007).

18. Neva Goodwin, "From Outer Circle to Center Stage: The Maturation of Heterodox Economics," 27–52, in *Future Directions for Heterodox Economics,* ed. John T. Harvey and Robert F. Garnett Jr. (Ann Arbor: University of Michigan Press, 2008). See also, Neva Goodwin, "Macroeconomics for the 21st Century," *Global Development and Environment Institute Working Paper No. 03–02* (Tufts University: February 2003).

19. Goodwin, "From Outer Circle to Center Stage," 30.

20. Ibid., 34.

21. Ibid., 35.

22. Bina Agarwal, "'Bargaining' and Gender Relations: Within and Beyond the Household," *Feminist Economics* 3, no. 1 (1997): 4.

23. Ibid., 23.

24. Martha Nussbaum, *Sex and Social Justice* (Oxford: Oxford University Press, 1999), 31.

25. Ibid., 19.

26. For example, see Marianne Hill, "Development as Empowerment," *Feminist Economics,* 9, no. 2/3 (July 2003): 117–35.

27. In contrast to the thesis that people are willing to forgo democratic liberties in favor of economic security, Sen cites examples such as South Korea, Thailand, Bangladesh, Pakistan, and Burma.

28. Amartya Sen, *Development as Freedom* (New York: Anchor Books, 1999), 146–59.

29. Joseph E. Stiglitz, "Democratizing the International Monetary Fund and the World Bank: Governance and Accountability," *Governance: An International Journal of Policy, Administration, and Institutions* 16, no. 1. (February 2003): 118.

30. Ibid., 120.

31. Timothy A. Wise and Kevin P. Gallagher, "Putting Development Back in the WTO," Global Development and Environment Institute, http://www.ase. tufts.edu/gdae/Pubs/rp/PuttingDevInWTODec08.pdf (accessed December 17, 2008): 16.

32. Mônica Dias Martins, "Learning to Participate: The MST Experience in Brazil," in *Promised Land: Competing Visions of Agrarian Reform*, ed. Peter Rosset, Raj Patel, and Michael Courville (Oakland: Food First Books, 2006), 268.

33. Carlo Petrini, *Slow Food: The Case for Taste*, trans. by William McCuaig (New York: Columbia University Press, 2001), 8.

34. Slow Food, "Slow Food," http://www.slowfood.com/ (accessed December 17, 2008).

35. Slow Food, "Linking Producers and Co-producers," http://www.slowfood. com/about_us/eng/linking_producers.lasso (accessed December 17, 2008).

36. Carlo Petrini, *Slow Food Nation: Why Our Food should be Good, Clean, and Fair*, trans. Clara Furlan and Jonathan Hunt (New York: Rizzoli Ex Libris, 2007), 55–88.

37. Jules Pretty, "Local Food: 'Greener' Than Organic," *BBC News*, March 2, 2005, http://news.bbc.co.uk/2/hi/science/nature/4312591.stm (accessed December 18, 2008)

38. Petrini, *Slow Food Nation*, 36.

39. Gun Roos, Laura Terragni and Hanne Torjusen, "The Local in the Global—Creating Ethical Relations between Producers and Consumers," *Anthropology of Food* 2 (March 2007), http://aof.revues.org/document489.html (accessed December 18, 2008).

40. Fair Trade Federation, "About Fair Trade," http://www.fairtradefedera tion.org/ht/d/sp/i/2733/pid/2733 (accessed April 24, 2009).

41. Laura T. Raynolds, "Re-embedding Global Agriculture: The International Organic and Fair Trade Movements," *Agriculture and Human Values* 17 (2000): 301.

42. Ibid., 301.

43. Ibid., 300.

44. World Fair Trade Organization, "Sixty Years of Fair Trade," http://www. wfto.com/index.php?option=com_content&task=view&id=10&Itemid=17 (accessed May 1, 2009).

45. Fair Trade Federation, "Facts and Figures," http://www.fairtradefedera tion.org/ht/d/sp/i/197/pid/197 (accessed May 1, 2009).

46. Oxfam, "Rigged Rules and Double Standards," http://www.maketrade fair.com/en/index.php?file=03042002121618.htm&cat=3&subcat=2&select=1 (accessed May 1, 2009).

47. Raynolds, "Re-embedding Global Agriculture," 299.

48. Ibid.

49. Ibid.

Bibliography

Agarwal, Bina. "'Bargaining' and Gender Relations: Within and Beyond the Household." *Feminist Economics* 3 no. 1 (1997): 1–51.

Altieri, Miguel A. "Agroecology: The Science of Natural Resource Management for Poor Farmers in Marginal Environments." *Agriculture, Ecosystems & Environment* 93, no. 9 (December 2002): 1–24.

Altieri, Miguel A. "Food Price Increases—Who Gets Hurt and What Can Be Done about It." *FoodFirst* 11 (April 2008), http://www.foodfirst.org/en/node/2084 (accessed January 6, 2008).

Altieri, Miguel A., Peter Rosset, and Ann Thrupp. "The Potential of Agroecology to Combat Hunger in the Developing World." *Policy Brief No. 55.* Washington, D.C.: IFPRI, 1998.

Bauer, Joanne R. and Daniel A. Bell, eds. *The East Asian Challenge for Human Rights.* Cambridge, MA: Cambridge University Press, 1999.

Bello, Walden. *Dark Victory: The United States and Global Poverty.* Oakland, CA: Food First Books, 1994.

Birdsall, Nancy, and John Nellis. "Winners and Losers: Assessing the Distributional Impact of Privatization." *World Development* 31, no. 10 (October 2003): 1617–33.

Borras Jr., Saturnino M. "The Underlying Assumptions, Theory and Practice of Neoliberal Land Policies." In *Promised Land: Competing Visions of Agrarian Reform,* edited by Peter Rosset, Raj Patel, and Michael Courville, 99–128. Oakland, CA: Food First Books, 2006.

Boucher, Doglas., ed. *The Paradox of Plenty: Hunger in a Bountiful World.* Oakland, CA: Food First Books, 1999.

Boudreaux, Karol, and Tyler Cowen. "The Micromagic of Microcredit." *Wilson Quarterly* 32, no. 1 (Winter 2008): 27–31.

Carlsen, Laura. "The Agrofuels Trap." *Americas Program Special Report* 11 (September 2007), http://americas.irc-online.org/am/4535 (accessed March 17, 2008).

CBC News, "Percy Schmeiser's Battle." (May 21, 2001), http://www.cbc.ca/news/background/genetics_modification/percyschmeiser.html (accessed February 27, 2008).

Collier, George A., and Elizabeth Quaratiello. *Basta!: Land and the Zapatista Rebellion in Chiapas.* 3rd ed. Oakland, CA: Food First Books, 2005.

Curio, Juana. "Seed at the Center of Food Sovereignty." *Seed Heritage of the People for the Good of Humanity.* http://viacampesina.org/main_en/images/stories/pdf/seed_heritage_of_the_people_for_the_good_of_humanity.pdf (accessed May 21, 2008).

Danaher, Kevin. *Ten Reasons to Abolish the IMF and World Bank.* 2nd ed. New York: Seven Stories Press, 2001.

Deininger, Klaus, and Hans Binswanger. "The Evolution of the World Bank's Land Policy." In *Access to Land, Rural Poverty, and Public Action,* edited by Alain De Janvry, Gustavo Gordillo, and Jean-Philippe Platteau, 406–40. Oxford: Oxford University Press, 2001.

De Palma, Anthony. "How a Tortilla Empire Was Built on Favoritism." *New York Times,* February 15, 1996.

De Shutter, Oliver. "New Production System Needed to Tackle Global Food Crisis, Says UN Expert." United Nations Press Release, October 16, 2008. http://www.unhchr.ch/huricane/huricane.nsf/view01/E196DCEE1E94E39DC12574E4002FC6CA?opendocument (accessed December 17, 2008).

De Wall, Alex. *Famine Crimes: Politics and the Disaster Relief Industry in Africa.* Bloomington: Indiana University Press, 1997.

Dowell-Jones, Mary. *Contextualizing the International Covenant on Economic, Social and Cultural Rights: Assessing the Economic Deficit.* Leiden/Boston: Martinus Nijhoff Publishers, 2004.

Dower, Glen A. *International Cooperation for Social Justice: Global and Regional Protection of Economic/Social Rights.* Westport, CT: Greenwood Press, 1985.

Elias, Paul, and Anne Fitzgerald. "Monsanto Sues Farmer Customers over Piracy Issues." *Des Moines Register* (January 30, 2005), http://www.mindfully.org/GE/2005/Monsanto-Sues-Farmers30jan05.htm (accessed February 27, 2008).

Erosion, Technology and Concentration Action Group (ETC Group). "Who Owns Nature? Corporate Power and the Final Frontier in the Commodification of Life." no. 100 (November 2008), http://www.etcgroup.org/en/materials/publications.html?pub_id=706 (accessed December 17, 2008).

Erosion, Technology and Concentration Action Group (ETC Group). "The World's Top Ten Seed Companies—2006." http://www.etcgroup.org/en/materials/publications.html?pub_id=656 (accessed April 3, 2008).

Fair Trade Federation. "About Fair Trade." http://www.fairtradefederation.org/ht/d/sp/i/2733/pid/2733 (accessed April 24, 2009).

Fair Trade Federation. "Facts and Figures." http://www.fairtradefederation.org/ht/d/sp/i/197/pid/197 (accessed May 1, 2009).

Fisher-Hoffman, Cory, Tessa Landreau-Brasmuck, Kaya Weidman, and Mandy Skinner. "The First Zapatista Women's Encuentro: A Collective Voice Of Resistance." (January 24, 2008), http://www.viacampesina.org/main_en/index.php?option=com_content&task=view&id=479&Itemid=39 (accessed May 28, 2008).

Follesdal, Andreas. "Human Rights and Relativism." In *Real World Justice*, edited by Andreas Follesdal, and Thomas Pogge, 265–83. The Netherlands: Springer, 2005.

Food and Agriculture Organization. "The State of Food and Agriculture 1996." http://www.fao.org/docrep/003/w1358e/w1358e00.htm (accessed April 3, 2008).

Food and Agriculture Organization. "FAO Tells WTO Meeting that Trade Liberalization Can Promote Food Security." http://www.fao.org/newsroom/en/news/2005/1000191/index.html (accessed April 3, 2008).

Food and Agriculture Organization. "The State of Food Insecurity in the World 2006." http://www.fao.org/docrep/009/a0750e/a0750e00.htm (accessed April 3, 2008).

Friedmann, Harriet. "Distance and Durability: Shaky Foundations of the World Food Economy." *Third World Quarterly* 13, no. 2 (June 1992): 371–83.

Friedmann, Harriet. "The International Political Economy of Food: A Global Crisis." In *Food in the USA: A Reader*, edited by Carele Counihan, 325–46. New York: Routledge, 2002.

Friedmann, Harriet. "Remaking 'Traditions': How We Eat, What We Eat and the Changing Political Economy of Food." In *Women Working the NAFTA Food Chain: Women, Food and Globalization*, edited by Deborah Barndt, 35–60. Toronto: Sumach Press, 1999.

Gerwith, Alan. *The Community of Rights*. Chicago: University of Chicago Press, 1996.

Gilabert, Pablo. "The Duty to Eradicate Global Poverty: Positive or Negative?" *Ethical Theory and Moral Practice* 7 no. 5 (November 2004): 537–50.

Goodwin, Neva. "From Outer Circle to Center Stage: The Maturation of Heterodox Economics." In *Future Directions for Heterodox Economics*, edited by John T. Harvey, and Robert F. Garnett Jr., 27–52. Ann Arbor: University of Michigan Press, 2008.

Goodwin, Neva. "Macroeconomics for the 21st Century." Global Development and Environment Institute Working Paper no. 03-02, Tufts University, February 2003.

Government Accountability Project (GAP). "Corruption Exposed at World Bank." (March 27, 2006), http://www.whistleblower.org/content/press_detail.cfm?press_id=408 (accessed February 11, 2008).

Hancock, Graham. *Lords of Poverty: The Power, Prestige, and Corruption of the International Aid Business*. New York: The Atlantic Monthly Press, 1989.

Harvey, Neil. "Rebellion in Chiapas: Rural Reforms and Popular Struggle." *Third World Quarterly* 16, no. 1 (March 1995): 39–73.

Hasan, Hamza. "Overview of U.S. Ethanol Market." Food First/Institute for Food and Development Policy. http://www.foodfirst.org/node/1723 (accessed March 17, 2008).

Hayden, Tom. *The Zapatista Reader*. New York: Thunder's Mouth Press, 2002.

Heffernan, William D., and Douglas H. Constance. "Transnational Corporations and the Globalization of the Food System." In *From Columbus to Con Agra: The Globalization of Agriculture and Food*, edited by Alessandro Bonanno et al., 29–51. Lawrence: University of Kansas Press, 1994.

Hill, Marianne. "Development as Empowerment." *Feminist Economics* 9, no. 2/3 (July 2003): 117–35.

Holt-Giménez, Eric. "The Biofuel Myths." *International Herald Tribune,* July, 10 2007. http://www.foodfirst.org/node/1716 (accessed March 17, 2008).

Holt-Giménez, Eric. "The Campesino a Campesino Movement: Farmer-led, Sustainable Agriculture in Central American and Mexico." In *The Paradox of Plenty: Hunger in a Bountiful World,* edited by Doglas Boucher, 297–314. Oakland, CA: Food First Books, 1999.

Holt-Giménez, Eric. *Campesino a Campesino: Voices from Latin America's Farmer to Farmer Movement for Sustainable Agriculture.* Oakland, CA: Food First Books, 2006.

Holt-Giménez, Eric. "U.S.-based Coalition Call for a Moratorium on U.S. Incentives for Biofuels." Food First. http://www.foodfirst.org/node/1811 (accessed March 17, 2008).

International Fund for Agricultural Development (IFAD). "About IFAD." http://www.ifad.org/governance/index.htm (accessed January 15, 2009).IFAD. "IFAD Strategy for Knowledge Management." http://www.ifad.org/gb-docs/eb/90/e/EB-2007-90-R-4.pdf (accessed February 15, 2008).

IFAD. "Rural Finance: From Unsustainable Projects to Sustainable Institutions for the Poor." http://www.ifad.org/pub/other/rural_e.pdf (accessed February 15, 2008).

IFAD. "A Summary of IFAD's Strategic Framework 2007–2010." http://www.ifad.org/governance/index.htm (accessed January 15, 2009).

International Monetary Fund (IMF). "IMF Surveillance." http://www.imf.org/external/np/exr/facts/surv.htm (accessed February 15, 2008).

IMF. "IMF Discusses Market Access for Developing Country Exports." http://www.imf.org/external/np/sec/pn/2002/pn02110.htm (accessed February 15, 2008).

IMF. "IMF Lending." http://www.imf.org/external/np/exr/facts/howlend.htm (accessed February 15, 2008).

IMF. "Technical Assistance." http://www.imf.org/external/np/exr/facts/tech.htm (accessed February 15, 2008).

International Monetary Fund and the World Bank. "Doha Development Agenda and Aid for Trade." http://www.imf.org/external/np/pp/eng/2005/091905.pdf (accessed March 4, 2009).

Ivanoe, Massimo. "The Universality of Human Rights and the International Protection of Cultural Diversity: Some theoretical and Practical Considerations." *International Journal on Minority and Group Rights* 14 (2007): 231–62.

Kimbrell, Andrew, and Joseph Mendelson. "Monsanto vs. U.S. Farmers: A Report by the Center for Food Safety." (Washington, D.C.: The Center for Food Safety, 2005), http://www.centerforfoodsafety.org/Monsantovsusfarmersreport.cfm (accessed March 10, 2008).

Kumar, Nagesh, and Kevin Gallagher. "Relevance of 'Policy Space' for Development: Implications for Multilateral Trade Negotiations." *Research and Information System for Developing Countries* no. 120 (New Delhi: India, 2007).

Langevin, Mark S., and Peter Rosset. "Land Reform from Below: The Landless Workers Movement in Brazil." In *The Paradox of Plenty: Hunger in a Bountiful World,* edited by Douglas Boucher, 323–29. Oakland, CA: Food First Books, 1999.

Lappé, Frances Moore, Joseph Collins, and Peter Rosset. *World Hunger: 12 Myths.* New York: Grove Press, 1998.

La Via Campesina. "The International Peasant's Voice." http://www.viacampesina. org/main_en/index.php?option=com_content&task=blogcategory&id=27 &Itemid=44 (accessed March 13, 2008).

Lind, David, and Elizabeth Barham. "The Social Life of the Tortilla: Food, Cultural Politics, and Contested Commodification." *Agriculture and Human Values* 21 (2004): 47–60.

Mander, Jerry. "Machine Logic: Industrializing Nature and Agriculture." In *The Fatal Harvest Reader: The Tragedy of Industrial Agriculture*, edited by Andrew Kimbrell, 87–91. Island Press: Foundation for Deep Ecology, 2002.

Maren, Michael. *The Road to Hell: The Ravaging Effects of Foreign Aid and International Charity*. New York: The Free Press, 1997.

Martins, Mônica Dias. "Learning to Participate: The MST Experience in Brazil." In *Promised Land: Competing Visions of Agrarian Reform*, edited by Peter Rosset, Raj Patel, and Michael Courville, 265–76. Oakland, CA: Food First Books, 2006.

McMichael, Philip. *Development and Social Change: A Global Perspective*, 2nd ed. Thousand Oaks, CA: Pine Forge Press, 2000.

McMichael, Philip. "Global Development and the Corporate Food Regime." In *New Directions in the Sociology of Global Development*, edited by Fredrick H. Buttel, and Philip McMichael, 265–300. Oxford: Elsevier, 2005.

McMichael, Philip. "The Power of Food." *Agriculture and Human Values* 17 (2000): 21–33.

Moe-Lobeda, Cynthia. *Healing a Broken World: Globalization and God*. Minneapolis, MN: Fortress Press, 2002.

MST. "About the MST." *Brazil's Landless Workers Movement*. http://www.mstbrazil. org/?q=about (accessed April 14, 2008).

MST. "Sectors and Collectives: How the MST Organizes Its Work, Gender Sector." *Brazil's Landless Workers Movement*. http://www.mstbrazil.org/?q=about (accessed April 14, 2008).

Navarro, Luis Hernández. "The New Tortilla War." *Americas Program Special Report*. Silver City, NM: International Relations Center, May 7, 2007.

Nussbaum, Martha. "Beyond the Social Contract." In *The Political Philosophy of Cosmopolitanism*, edited by Gillian Brock, and Harry Brighouse, 196–218. Cambridge, MA: Cambridge University Press, 2005.

Nussbaum, Martha. "Capabilities as Fundamental Entitlements: Sen and Social Justice." *Feminist Economics* 9, no. 2 (July 2003): 33–59.

Nussbaum, Martha. "Capabilities and Human Rights," *Fordham Law Review* 66 (1997): 273–300.

Nussbaum, Martha. "Poverty and Human Functioning: Capabilities as Fundamental Entitlements." In *Poverty and Inequality*, edited by David B. Grusky, and Ravi Kanbur, 47–75. Stanford, CA: Stanford University Press, 2006.

Nussbaum, Martha. *Sex and Social Justice*. Oxford: Oxford University Press, 1999.

Ochoa, Enrique C. *Feeding Mexico: The Political Uses of Food since 1910*. Wilmington, DE: Scholarly Resources Books, 2000.

Organic Consumers Association. "Monsanto's Government Ties." http://www.or ganicconsumers.org/monlink.cfm#monsanto (accessed January 22, 2008).

Oxfam. "Rigged Rules and Double Standards." http://www.maketradefair.com/ en/index.php?file=03042002121618.htm&cat=3&subcat=2&select=1 (accessed May 1, 2009).

PANNA. "Corporate Profile: Monsanto Company." http://www.panna.org/re
    sources/caia/corpProfilesMonsanto (accessed January 17, 2008).
Patel, Raj. *Stuffed and Starved: The Hidden Battle for the World Food System*. Brooklyn,
    New York: Melville House Publishing, 2007.
Patel, Raj. "Critical Themes in Agrarian Reform." In *Promised Land: Competing Vi-
    sions of Agrarian Reform*, edited by Peter Rosset, Raj Patel, and Michael Cour-
    ville, 95–98. Oakland, CA: Food First Books, 2006.
Patel, Raj, and Gisele Henriques. "Agricultural Trade Liberalization and Mexico."
    Food First Policy Brief No. 7. Oakland, CA: Food First Institute for Food and
    Development Policy, 2003.
Patel, Rajeev, Radhika Balakrishnan, and Uma Nayaran. "Explorations on Human
    Rights." *Feminist Economics* 13, no. 1 (January 2007): 87–116.
Petrik, Will. "COHA's Analysis of the IMF and IDB Part 1." *The Guatemala Times*,
    April 23, 2009. http://www.guatemala-times.com/news/world/1047-co
    haas-analysis-of-the-imf-and-the-idb-part-1.html (accessed July 1, 2009).
Petrini, Carlo. *Slow Food: The Case for Taste*. Translated by William McCuaig. New
    York: Columbia University Press, 2001.
Petrini, Carlo. *Slow Food Nation: Why our Food Should be Good, Clean, and Fair*. Trans-
    lated by Clara Furlan, and Jonathan Hunt. New York: Rizzoli Ex Libris,
    2007.
Phillips, Lynne. "Food and Globalization." *Annual Review of Anthropology* 35 (2006):
    37–57.
Pinstrup-Anderson, Per, and Peter Sandøe, eds. *Ethics, Hunger and Globalization: In
    Search of Appropriate Policies*. Dordrecht, The Netherlands: Springer, 2007.
Pogge, Thomas. "A Cosmopolitan Perspective on the Global Economic Order." In
    The Political Philosophy of Cosmopolitanism, edited by Gillian Brock, and Harry
    Brighouse, 92–109. Cambridge, MA: Cambridge University Press, 2005.
Pogge, Thomas. "The First UN Millennium Development Goal: A Cause for Cel-
    ebration?" In *Real World Justice*, edited by Andreas Follesdal and Thomas
    Pogge, 317–338. Dordrecht, The Netherlands: Springer, 2005.
Pogge, Thomas. "Real World Justice." *The Journal of Ethics* 9 (2005): 29–53.
Pogge, Thomas. *World Poverty and Human Rights*. Malden, MA: Blackwell Publish-
    ers Inc, 2002.
Pound, Edward T., and Danielle Knight. "Cleaning up the World Bank." *U.S. News
    and World Report*, March 26, 2006. http://www.usnews.com/usnews/biz
    tech/articles/060403/3worldbank.htm (accessed February 11, 2008).
Pretty, Jules. "Local food: 'Greener' than Organic" *BBC News*, March 2, 2005. http://
    news.bbc.co.uk/2/hi/science/nature/4312591.stm (accessed December 18,
    2008).
Prichard, Bill, and Robert Fagan. "Circuits of Capital and Transnational Corporate
    Spatial Behaviour: Nestle in Southeast Asia." *International Journal of Sociology
    of Agriculture and Food* 8 (1999): 3–20.
Quintana, Victor. "Biofuels and Small Farmers." *America's Program*. http://americas.
    irc-online.org/am/4510 (accessed February 10, 2009).
Rawls, John. *Justice as Fairness: A Restatement*. Cambridge, MA: Harvard University
    Press, 2001.
Raynolds, Laura T. "Re-embedding Global Agriculture: The International Or-
    ganic and Fair Trade Movements." *Agriculture and Human Values* 17 (2000):
    297–309.

Renteln, Alison. "Relativism and the Search for Human Rights." *American Anthropologist* 90, no. 1 (March 1988): 56–72.

Roos, Gun, Laura Terragni, and Hanne Torjusen. "The Local in the Global—Creating Ethical Relations Between Producers and Consumers." *Anthropology of Food* 2 (March 2007), http://aof.revues.org/document489.html (accessed December 18, 2008).

Rosset, Peter. *Food is Different: Why We Must Get the WTO Out of Agriculture.* Nova Scotia: Fernwood Publishing, 2006.

Rosset, Peter. "The Multiple Functions and Benefits of Small Farm Agriculture: In the Context of Global Trade Negotiations." *Food First Policy Brief No. 4.* Oakland, CA: Food First Institute for Food and Development Policy, 1999.

Rosset, Peter. "The U.S. Opposes Right to Food at World Summit." *Food First* (June 30, 2002), http://www.foodfirst.org/archive/media/opeds/2002/usopposes.html (accessed February 27, 2008).

Rosset, Peter. "The U.S. Opposes the Right to Food at World Summit." http://www.mindfully.org/Food/Right-To-Food30jun02.htm (accessed March 4, 2009).

Rosset, Peter, Raj Patel, and Michael Courville. *Promised Land: Competing Visions of Agrarian Reform.* Oakland, CA: Food First Books, 2006.

Sachs, Jeffrey. *The End of Poverty: Economic Possibilities for Our Time.* New York: Penguin Books, 2005.

Selby, David. *Human Rights.* Cambridge, MA: Cambridge University Press, 1987.

Sen, Amartya. *Development as Freedom.* New York: Anchor Books, 1999.

Sen, Amartya. "Idea of Justice." *Journal of Human Development* 9, no. 3 (November 2008): 331–42.

Sen, Amartya. *Inequality Reexamined.* Cambridge, MA: Harvard University Press, 1992.

Sethi, Manpreet. "Land Reform in India: Issues and Challenges." In *Promised Land: Competing Visions of Agrarian Reform,* edited by Peter Rosset, Raj Patel, and Michael Courville, 73–92. Oakland, CA: Food First Books, 2006.

Shand, Hope J. "Intellectual Property: Enhancing Corporate Monopoly and Bioserfdom." In *The Fatal Harvest Reader: The Tragedy of Industrial Agriculture,* edited by Andrew Kimbrell, 240–48. Washington: Island Press, 2002.

Shiva, Vandana, ed. *Manifestos on the Future of Food and Seed.* Cambridge, MA: South End Press, 2007.

Shiva, Vandana, ed. "Microcredit: Solution to Poverty or False 'Compassionate Capitalism?'" *Democracy Now* (December 12, 2006), http://www.democracynow.org/2006/12/13/microcredit_solution_to_poverty_or_false (accessed March 3, 2008).

Shiva, Vandana, "Shiva Responds to the Grameen Bank." *Synthesis/Regeneration* 17 (1998), http://www.greens.org/s-r/17/17-15.html (accessed January 25, 2008).

Shiva, Vandana, *Stolen Harvest: The Hijacking of the Global Food Supply.* Cambridge, MA: South End Press, 2000.

Shiva, Vandana, "War Against Nature and the People of the South." In *Views from the South: The effects of globalization and the WTO on third world countries,* edited by Sarah Anderson, 91–125. Oakland, CA: Food First Books, 2000.

Singer, Peter. "Famine, Affluence, and Morality." *Philosophy and Public Affairs* 1, no. 3 (Spring 1972): 229–43. Princeton, NJ: Princeton University Press.

Sixth Declaration of the Selva Lacandona, anarkismo.net http://www.anarkismo.net/newswire.php?story_id=805 (accessed February 10, 2009).

Slow Food. "Linking Producers and Co-producers." http://www.slowfood.com/about_us/eng/linking_producers.lasso (accessed December 17, 2008).

Slow Food. "Slow Food." http://www.slowfood.com/ (accessed December 17, 2008).

Smaller, Cairn. "Planting the Rights Seed: A Human Rights Perspective on Agriculture Trade and the WTO." Institute for Agriculture and Trade Policy, Backgrounder no. 1. Minneapolis, MN: 2005.

Spector, Rebecca. "Fully Integrated Food Systems: Regaining Connections between Farmers and Consumers." In *The Fatal Harvest Reader: The Tragedy of Industrial Agriculture*, edited by Andrew Kimbrel, 288–94. Washington: Island Press, 2002.

Staples, Amy L. *The Birth of Development: How the World Bank, Food and Agriculture Organization, and World Health Organization Changed the World, 1945–1965.* Kent, OH: The Kent State University Press, 2006.

Stiglitz, Joseph E. "Democratizing the International Monetary Fund and the World Bank: Governance and Accountability." *Governance: An International Journal of Policy, Administration, and Institutions* 16, no. 1 (February 2003): 111–39.

Stiglitz, Joseph E. *Globalization and its Discontents*. New York: W. W. Norton & Company, 2003.

Tripathy, Ruchi. "Implications of TRIPs on Livelihoods of Poor Farmers in Developing Countries." *ActionAid* 13 (October 2000), http://www.actionaid.org.uk/content_document.asp?doc_id=240 (accessed January 17, 2008).

UNESCO. "Declaration on Cultural Diversity." Paris, France (2001). Also available at http://unesdoc.unesco.org/images/0012/001271/127160m.pdf.

United Nations. "Declaration of Human Rights." http://un.org/Overview/rights.html#a6 (accessed December 17, 2008).

United Nations. "Economic, Social and Cultural Rights: The Right to Food," *Economic and Social Council*. E/CN.4/2004/10 (February 9, 2004), http://www.unhchr.ch/huridocda/huridoca.nsf/(Symbol)/E.CN.4.2004.10.En (accessed December 17, 2008).

United Nations. "International Covenant on Economic, Social and Cultural Rights." http://www.unhchr.ch/html/menu3/b/a_cescr.htm (accessed December 17, 2008).

United Nations. "New Production System Needed to Tackle Global Food Crisis, Says UN Expert" Press Release, October 16, 2008, http://www.unhchr.ch/huricane/huricane.nsf/view01/E196DCEE1E94E39DC12574E4002FC6CA?opendocument (accessed December 17, 2008).

United Nations. "Vienna Declaration and Programme of Action." Vienna (June 1993): 14–25.

United Nations Development Program (UNDP). "Millennium Development Goals: A Compact Among Nations to End Human Poverty." *Human Development Report 2003.* New York: Oxford University Press, 2003.

United States. "Fact Sheet: Energy Independence and Security Act of 2007." http://georgewbush-whitehouse.archives.gov/news/releases/2007/12/20071219-1.html (accessed February 21, 2009).

Victor M. Quintana S. "Biofuels and Small Farmers." *Americas Program Policy Brief* (Washington, D.C.: Center for International Policy, August 29, 2007), http://americas.irc-online.org/am/4510 (accessed March 17, 2008).

Waters, Alice. "The Ethics of Eating: Why Environmentalism Starts at the Breakfast Table." In *The Fatal Harvest Reader: The Tragedy of Industrial Agriculture,* edited by Andrew Kimbrell, 283–87. Washington, D.C.: Island Press, 2002.

Weisbrot, Mark, Dean Baker, Robert Naiman, and Gila Neta. "Growth May Be Good for the Poor—But are IMF and World Bank Policies Good for Growth?" Center for Economic and Policy Research, http://www.cepr.net/index.php?option=com_content&task=view&id=427 (accessed February 15, 2008).

Weston, Burns H. "The Universality of Human Rights in a Multicultured World." In *Human Rights in the World Community: Issues and Action,* 3rd ed., edited by Richard Pierre Claude, and Burns H. Weston. Philadelphia: University of Pennsylvania Press, 2006.

Windfuhr, Michael, and Jennie Jonsén. *Food Sovereignty: Towards Democracy in Localised Food Systems.* United Kingdom: ITDG Publishing, 2005.

Wise, Timothy A., and Kevin P. Gallagher. "Putting Development Back in the WTO," Global Development and Environment Institute, http://www.ase.tufts.edu/gdae/Pubs/rp/PuttingDevInWTODec08.pdf (accessed December 17, 2008).

The World Bank. "Reaching the Rural Poor: A Renewed Strategy for Rural Development." Washington, D.C., 2002.

The World Bank. "World Development Report 2008: Agriculture for Development." Washington, D.C., 2008.

World Fair Trade Organization, "Sixty Years of Fair Trade." http://www.wfto.com/index.php?option=com_content&task=view&id=10&Itemid=17 (accessed May 1, 2009).

World Food Summit: Rome Declaration on World Food Security. Rome (November 1996): 13–17. http://www.fao.org/docrep/003/w3613e/w3613e00.HTM (accessed December 11, 2008).

World Trade Organization (WTO). "6th Ministerial Conference, Hong Kong, December 15, 2005, Statement by Food and Agricultural Organization of the United Nations." http://www.fao.org/newsroom/en/news/2005/1000191/index.html (accessed January 31, 2008).

WTO. "The Doha Development Agenda." (2007a). http://www.wto.org/english/thewto_e/whatis_e/whatis_e.htm (accessed January 2, 2008).

WTO. "Domestic Support in Agriculture: The Boxes." (2001b). http://www.wto.org/english/tratop_e/agric_e/agboxes_e.htm (accessed January 2, 2008).

WTO. "Ministerial Declaration." WT/MIN(01)/DEC/1 (2001c). http://www.wto.org/english/thewto_e/minist_e/min01_e/min01_e.htm (accessed January 2, 2008).

WTO. "Ten Benefits of the WTO Trading System." (2007d). http://www.wto.org/english/thewto_e/whatis_e/10ben_e/10b00_e.htm (accessed January 2, 2008).

WTO. "Understanding the WTO: The Agreements. Intellectual Property: Protection and Enforcement." (2007e). http://www.wto.org/english/thewto_e/whatis_e/tif_e/agrm7_e.htm (accessed January 2, 2008).

WTO. "WTO Programme on Aid-for-Trade." WT/AFT/W/26 (2007f). http://www.wto.org/english/tratop_e/devel_e/a4t_e/aid4trade_e.htm (accessed January 2, 2008).

WTO. "What is the WTO?" http://www.wto.org/english/thewto_e/whatis_e/whatis_e.htm (accessed January 2, 2008).

Wright, Angus, and Wendy Wolford. "Now is the Time: The MST and Grassroots Land Reform in Brazil." Food First Backgrounder 9, no. 2 (Spring 2003). Oakland, CA: Food First, 2003.

Index

About the Author

WILLIAM D. SCHANBACHER holds a PhD in Religion from Claremont Graduate University, a Master of Theological Studies from Duke Divinity School, and a BA in Economics and History from the University of Colorado. His primary area of research is in social and religious ethics with a focus on the intersection between ethics, religion, economics, politics, human rights, and social justice movements, both in the United States and globally. He currently lives and teaches in Denver, Colorado.